DEDICATIONS

A mother's love is surpassed only by God's love.

Without the fullness of love and support of my mother Mrs. Irene Wilder this book would not have been possible. Thank you momma!

D.E. WILDER

ANATOMY OF STYLE

The ULTIMATE GUIDE to HARNESS the POWER of your PERSONAL PRESENTATION

ROCK HEAD PRESS  NEW YORK

www.anatomy-of-style.com

ANATOMY OF STYLE

Anyone can buy fashion, but all the money in the world cannot buy you style. Remember that!

Published in 2011 by Rock Head Press
An imprint of DEW Publishing Group, USA

Copyright © 2010 by D.E. Wilder

Cover photo: © courtesy of Casare Attolini, Naples
All rights reserved

PHOTO CREDITS:

p 5.© courtesy of Oxxford Clothes, p 6,100. © courtesy of Casare Attolini, Naples , p 9,13,21,48,52,93. © courtesy of Tom Ford, p 11. © courtesy of Conde Nast, p 12,95. © courtesy of Hackett, p 14,28,35,36,38,51,53,74. © courtesy of Paul Stuart, p 8,17,18,19,25,27,33,34,46. © courtesy of Robb Report, p 22,24,45,57,71,79,82,84,85,87,93,98,99,104,113. © courtesy of Domenico Vacca, p 23. © courtesy of Vincent Van Gogh, p 41. © courtesy Marc Jacobs, p37. © courtesy of Terrice Love, p 43. © courtesy of Maya Guez Photography, p 43. © courtesy of Mitchell Feinberg Photography, p 44. © courtesy of E.D. Salisbury, p 56. © courtesy of Michael Scott Jones, p 59,78,91. © courtesy of Martin Kenneth, p 64,69,97. © courtesy of Ralph Lauren, p 66. © courtesy of Pal Zileri, p 49. © courtesy of Nautica, p53,110,112. © courtesy of Isaia, p 72. © courtesy of Sophia Wallace, p 70,73. © courtesy of Corneliani, p 108,116. © courtesy of B. Oyama

All rights reserved. No portion of this book may be reproduced, stored in a retrieval system, or transmitted in any form or by any means, mechanical, electronic, photocopying, recording, or otherwise, without written permission from the publisher.

Library of Congress Cataloging-in-Publication Data:
Anatomy of Style / D.E. Wilder.
p. cm.
ISBN-13: 978-0-61562-180-7
ISBN-10:   0-61562-180-5
1. Success-----Psychological aspects. 2. Men's Clothing.
I. Wilder, Desmond. II. Title.

Editor: Kenneth Salikof
Designer: Rock Head Group
Production Manager: The DEW Group

The text of this book was composed in Sans Serif, Copperplate Gothic and Calibri

Printed and bound in United States of America

10 9 8 7 6 5 4 3 2 1

Rock Head Press books are available at special discounts when purchased in quantity for premiums and promotions as well as fundraising or educational use. Special editions can also be created to specification.

Contents

INTRODUCTION	VI
ANATOMY OF MY STYLE	10
CENTERPIECE OF STYLE	17
FOUNDATION OF STYLE	23
COUNTERPART OF STYLE	32
CROWN JEWEL OF STYLE	40
CUSTOMIZATION OF STYLE	45
TIMEKEEPER OF STYLE	56
CASUALTY OF STYLE	64
WORLD OF STYLE	70
PSYCHOLOGY OF STYLE	78
VOICE OF STYLE	86
APPEARANCE OF STYLE	102
GUIDELINE OF STYLE	108
SIDE-STEP OF STYLE	112
ACKNOWLEDGEMENTS	117
INDEX	118
RESOURCE GUIDE	120

INTRODUCTION

This book is for any man who is interested in perfecting his own personal style, because the very essence of style is very personal and subjective; in other words, the style that works for you may not work for me and vice versa. Style and fashion always seem to go together, like a hand in a glove. Nevertheless, I believe when it comes to men and clothing, it should be about style, which should have nothing to do with fashion. As a man, if you follow the latest fashion trends you may end up looking ridiculous, because every style and every designer's cut are not going to work for you. However, if you focus on your own personal style, then you can always incorporate some of the latest designer's garments into your pre-existing wardrobe. Once you find your own personal style, I promise that you will always know what to wear on any occasion and look good at the same time.

STYLE THAT FITS YOU!

Dressing well always comes down to fit; wearing clothing that compliments your physique should be the ultimate look you are seeking. The only way you could get away with wearing anything from any designer is to be the size of one of those Calvin Klein models up on some billboard, and we all know that is not the case for most of us; so we reverse the strategy and change the focus to finding what fits your stature and works for your size as well as shape. Whether you are big and tall or short and thin, you can dress well every day while being neat and comfortable in your clothes.

Let us get down to business; Rome was not built overnight and neither will your wardrobe. Finding your style will take some time; because only in time will you find the right pieces to compliment your build. Therefore, unless you are a millionaire with a personal stylist or designer, be patient in building your wardrobe. This will save you from many costly, unwanted and unworn garments.

Here is one of the main ingredients of dressing well: maintenance; it will always come down to how well you take care of your suits, how maintained you keep your shoes and how carefully you pressed your shirts. If you maintain your wardrobe, which should consist of choice quality garments (not quantity), you will see how a little can truly go a long way.

THE BIG C RULE!

In this book, the first of an entire series that will break down the anatomy of style, I will focus on what I call the soul of style, which are all the elements you will need to find your personal style. Accessories truly accentuate anything you are wearing, regardless of how vast or small your wardrobe may be. So I will focus on the most essential pieces, such as shoes, socks, and belts, helping you best utilize these style enhancers. Then I will move on to ties, cufflinks and hats; these essentials will embellish your wardrobe, so keep an open mind and be creative. I will also cover the etiquette of wearing jewelry and how to select the perfect timepiece.

Be prepared to have a good time exploring the considerable options and opportunities of finding your own personal style. The first rule of thumb you should try to remember throughout this book is to always be comfortable; there is no reason you should look your best but be uncomfortable all day. The second rule of thumb is confidence. I am going to tell you an ancient secret: if you are comfortable and confident you can wear anything and make it look cool. This leads me to the third rule of thumb: you must always be cool. Understanding the three C's rule will help you achieve your goal much quicker.

THREE C's RULE

Comfortable

Confident

Cool

LET'S GET STARTED!

I'm not sure if we really want to call shoes an accessory, but they are the single most important complement to anything you could wear. The right pair of shoes is the icing on the cake of any wardrobe; your shoes will complete your look. In recent years we have seen a huge movement towards dress-down work environments promoting relaxed business casual attire. For those of you who enjoy the privilege of working, but not having the prerequisite to complement your duties with professional attire, kudos to you. But there are some of us who know that dressing the part is only half the job. If you had to be represented by an attorney and he or she walked into the room wearing khakis and a pullover sweater, I sincerely doubt you would be brimming with confidence in his/her ability to get the job done. Dressing appropriately is part and parcel of any job, and it's a key element when it comes to being successful. You need not be a lawyer for this to apply.

While this dress-down movement raged on, I have seen the most hideous combinations of suits and shoes for both men and women. I think to myself "Don't they know you can't do that?" The shoes are the foundation of any outfit. You can test this for yourself. Put on your best outfit with your best pair of shoes to compliments that outfit, and then try on a pair of sneakers or rubber soled walking shoes with the same outfit. I can guarantee that it will no longer be your best outfit; the entire effect will be lost, all by not wearing the most complimentary shoes. Wearing the wrong pair of shoes is death to a wardrobe.

Let's get this party started right, because it's not hard to dress well every day in any occasion when you know what works for **YOU**.

THE ANATOMY OF MY STYLE

There has always been an importance to having a well-dressed appearance to me, but I must admit for me it has always been all about style. Growing up I couldn't afford fashion, but I was always able to create style. Style is an art, and being stylish is at the heart of creativity and self-expression; and you are going to need some real creativity to conjure something out of nothing. When I was young, my home was flowing with creativity. I was the youngest of five boys in a household where there was always something going on and there was never a dull moment to be found.

My mother was a stickler for proper hygiene and made certain that we were always looking, as she called it, "presentable." We did not have much money, especially extra disposable funds to purchase the latest fashion. And I don't know how my mother did it, because we were always some of the best-dressed kid in the neighborhood. My mother was a master at creating something from nothing; she would put together for each of us exceptional outfits consisting of hand-me-downs, goodwill and some new pieces of clothes. When we walked out the door as a family, we were always photo ready. This is a true testament to my mother's creativity and her ability to make a lot from a little, while making it all look easy.

I must admit as I grew into a young man, my style went through a true metamorphosis, a full range of style transformations. I experimented with many looks, ranging from my Sunday suits to the all-black Goth look; yes, I had the keys and chain hanging from the pocket, as well, and I was fully committed to the look. As a person with a lot of creativity, I really did not have an appreciation for style expressions at that stage of my development, which is probably common with most teenagers.

REMEMBERING!

My mother always stressed to me that one should look presentable at all times and be ready for anything continuously. I come to surround my life with those fundamental principles, which is the anatomy of my style.

THE GQ LOOK!

I remember clear as day, it was around the age of fourteen that I discovered *GQ* magazine; my mother had purchased a copy for one of my uninterested older brothers and I picked it up and read it from cover to cover. This was not only a pivotal moment for me in the development of my own style, but it was a pivotal time for the magazine as well. In the mid – 80's, Art Cooper took the helms as Editor-in-Chief of *GQ* magazine. During his tenure, the publication truly established itself as the authority of all things fashion as it pertained to men. Each month, on full display, was the finest menswear money could buy and the fashion editorial was unparallel by any other publication on this topic. The styles displayed became the standard by which most well-dressed men sought to aspire to. During Mr. Cooper's editorial leadership the term "you look *GQ*" was established.

Being so young, I could only dream of wearing anything displayed within those pages; fact is, I couldn't even afford a pair of socks on the editorial pages. But I could dream, and dream I did. What *GQ* magazine taught me was how to put together a great looking outfit. It was about choosing quality pieces and not about everything matching or the names on the label. I discovered the importance of finding the right article of clothing that can stand on its own within your entire wardrobe. The most important lesson I learned was: although the publisher showed the best designers in the world with the price tag to match, I discovered you didn't need to have the best designer names to have the *GQ* look--you just needed to know how to put it together.

GQ Magazine
Eddie Murphy
July 1992

Art Cooper
GQ Editor-in-chief
1983 - 2003

WHERE TO FIND YOUR UNIQUENESS!

At that point I shifted my focus from wanting to be fashionable to being stylish and expressing my own sense of style. I did not shop around seeking designers' names at all. I was on a mission to find excellent pieces to add to my wardrobe and they had to be unique, stylishly me and make me feel good. And it had to be unique so no one else could duplicate this style. I discovered this all before the age of eighteen. Once I started working and making my own money, it was on. I knew what to wear, how to wear it and when to wear it, so now I just needed to find out where to buy it. For me, shopping in a department store didn't cut it. I found that shopping at a men's shop would provide me with the one-of-a-kind look that became paramount for my style. There is nothing wrong with shopping at a department store, because no one can match their selection or inventory. But I created a system to my shopping routine, which taught me how to shop, where to shop and how to save money. Here is my system:

DEPARTMENT STORE

Coats
Sweaters
Suits (sometime)
Socks

SPECIALTY SHOP

Suits
Shirts
Ties

MEN'S BOUTIQUE

Shoes
Cufflinks
Pocket Handkerchief
Trousers

SHOP AROUND!

As you can see, with my system the number one key is to shop around and never purchase an entire outfit in one place. This will allow for a uniqueness in your look and it will save you money in the end, because shopping around will give you the opportunity to price survey and determine what you get for the money.

I have a firm belief that anyone, if they can afford it, can buy fashion. But having all the money in the world cannot buy you style. Style is developed over time and you must shop around to nurture your style's growth. There are aspects of your style that you will eliminate and come to terms with the fact that you have outgrown some things (i.e. bowties, pink shirts and sleeveless cardigans) and there are elements of your style that you will enhance and come to appreciate unique essentials of good taste. Therefore you will always be on a quest to reinvent your wardrobe. And this is a good thing because you want to always keep your look fresh and clean.

WALL STREET POWER LOOK!

It was my Wall Street days that set my style on fire; at this stage, money wasn't an object, so style was overpowering and dramatic. It was the era of power everything--power ties, power suits, and the infamous power lunch. Everything was done in a grand fashion and style was no exception. I can remember so vividly how I perfected the ties and braces combination. I had just as many pair of braces as ties. Since there's an art to finding the most unique and exceptional pair of braces, in those days I was like a contemporary artist putting together a wardrobe that was nothing short of masterful. But in my early days on Wall Street, it was all about how you looked and who was looking at you; it was a lot of flash and wearing your wealth on your sleeve. No matter how well I looked in those days, I still did not find the DNA of my style until some years later.

BRIGHT BEGINNINGS!

The anatomy of my style is fueled by all the fashion trials and errors I've experience through my never-ending quest to be at my best. All the clothing that did not fit well, all the poor quality garments that did not last longer than several wearing were all affectionately attributable to the development of the admired style that I grace the world with today. I had to learn over time what makes me comfortable and what cuts as well as colors were the fundamental elements that would allow me to create a style that celebrates all of my natural qualities and allows me continuously to be at my best.

CENTERPIECE OF STYLE

"Common sense is genius dressed up in work clothes".
- Ralph Waldo Emerson

"A true styles-man makes the time to press them himself. Pressing a shirt is like washing your car: when you wash it by hand yourself, it feels a little more gratifying to drive."

Your shirt is single-handedly the most versatile piece of garment you can put on your back. So let us explore why this is so and the benefit of choosing the perfect pressed shirt. I like to call what we wear every day our uniform, so I will break down the uniform like this. The suit or sport jacket and slacks are your mainstay outer shell; this is constant and should be maintained to the highest ends. But what really makes what you wear come to life are your shirts and shoes; these elements will always be the main focus of anything you are wearing.

The large variety of shirt options is truly unlimited; the choices include fabrics, patterns, collars, buttons, cuffs, and, of course, colors. When you get to the point where you can no longer find the shirts that will tickle your fancy, it seems to me like you are ready for a custom shirt maker, where the options are even more liberal. But let's not get ahead of ourselves.

You can start by choosing the pattern family that you are interested in, whether stripes, checks or solid colors are what you like; I suggest you explore all options. Now you want to select the feel/fabric, which ranges from fine Egyptian cotton to double-woven cotton that will feel heavier. There are also premium imperial cotton, and supple Italian cotton.

The entire logic behind the shirt being the centerpiece of your wardrobe is you can wear the same suits or sport jackets each week but with a different shirt. Not only would this be unnoticeable, but also it would appear to some that you are wearing a different suit. Yes, your shirts can make a huge difference; moreover, if you add an outstanding tie and the right belt, you will look exceptional no matter the day or the hour. The most important ingredient after selecting the right shirts for your wardrobe is you must be sure they are well pressed; wrinkled shirts are not an option. Whether you have your shirts starch or no starch from the laundry, they must be pressed well. A true styles-man makes the time to press them himself. Pressing a shirt is like washing your car: when you wash it by hand yourself, it feels a little more gratifying to drive. You'll feel the difference, trust me.

Your look should work together!

Even the tie and shirt combination will make a strong impact; keep in mind that the principle behind the shirt centerpiece theory is to save you money, because you shouldn't have to buy a new suit every couple of month. A good suit can last for many fun-filled useful years, but only under one condition: you must properly maintain it and consistently refresh it. The best way to refresh a suit is to steam-press it. It helps if you have your own streamer. But if you are not so lucky, you can make do by hanging your suit on the door in your bathroom as you take a hot shower. If this all sounds too time consuming, it's not; it will become second nature once you put it into everyday practice.

SIDEBAR: Mark Twain once said, "clothes make the man". This is only a true statement if you are a man without style. Simply put, anyone if they can afford it could buy an expensive piece of clothing. But it is only the man with a personal sense of style that can bring those clothes to life.

When it comes to neckties, you have an unlimited number of options, far beyond those of shirts selection even. This is the single most distinctive way a person can express his sartorial individuality. You can let your personality shine through when selecting your ties or you can be conservative and play it safe with a paisley (which is timeless) or repetitive pattern tie. What you should always remember is: don't be afraid to let your tie become a conversation piece. It can really work well if you are in Sales or Marketing, because people seem to respond enthusiastically to a superior tie.

I have some great examples of standout shirt and suit combinations, as well as tie and shirt collaborations. Remember to keep up with your freshly pressed shirts; this will single-handedly boost the profile of your entire wardrobe. This can even work for the casual every day guy as well. If you seldom wear a tie, then having a great shirt collection is that much more important.

Two things will most certainly ruin any outfit, poor looking shoes that are not maintained well and an unpressed shirt. I would define some outstanding patterns and designs of shirts, but in keeping with letting your own personality shine through and establishing your own style I will encourage you to go with any design or pattern that makes you feel good just as long as the shirt is well pressed. Crisp and clean is the golden rule.

STYLE-TRADEMARK!

I want every man to explore his own personal style to the point where it will become your **Style-Trademark**. Here is a good indication: when your style becomes your trademark to the degree that the people around you start to spruce-up their wardrobes to be at par with yours, you will know that you have achieved a consistent clean style that is respected and admired by others. Another thing to note, for truly stylish men: if the people who see you often compliment you on your dressing, then you haven't cemented your style as of yet: only at the point when no one notices, but it's just expected, will you know that your style has been set. By the way, compliments from strangers are certainly welcome.

FOUNDATION OF STYLE
A Pair of Shoes 1887
(Vincent van Gogh)

"The shoe is the grand finale when it comes to completing your wardrobe."

It's a shoo-in!

There is nothing wrong with taking inspiration for a certain style from a men's boutique window display or from the pages of a menswear ad, or even another stylish person, just so long as you make it your own and do not duplicate it to a tee. Remember fashion is copied all the time, but style can never be duplicated; as a constant reminder, your goal is to create what style work best for you.

If the shirt is the centerpiece of the wardrobe, then your shoes are the cherry on the sundae. The shoe is the grand finale when it comes to completing your wardrobe. Before we get down to the business of developing your style, I want to make it perfectly clear that unlike our female counterparts, comfort is the absolute most important concern above and beyond all else. Also, if you had health-related issues with your feet, then you should choose the best footwear that will address those concerns.

SIDEBAR: Classic style is never out of style; so you can always include braces into your wardrobe every once in a while. Braces adds a touch of distinction.

25

Now, for the rest of us, please do not put on a pair of rubber soled walking shoes with a super 120's Italian tailored suit; this is one of the most awful assaults to the eye. The shoes you choose make or break not only your outfit, but also your entire wardrobe if not paired correctly with each outfit. For this reason, most stylish gentlemen have different shoes for different styles of dress. Shoes come in a wide variety of styles, shapes, and skin colors. You can purchase quality shoes from a men's boutique or department store, but if you want to be in a class of your own, than you can have a custom made pair of shoes taken from a mold of your foot. But let's not get ahead of ourselves.

I find for the most part that the type and price a man is willing to pay for his shoes often go hand in hand with his income level; I am not talking styling, but I am speaking to quality and cost. Men with a higher income level tend to spend more on higher quality of footwear than those with lower income levels, and I think this is the way it should be. As you work toward getting that corner office, you can also work towards getting custom hand-made shoes; this is one of the spoils of being on top.

The average price for a good shoe is $200.00, but for the manufacturers with long-standing reputations and old world construction techniques, that price can easily rise above $500.00. My advice in this area is price makes all the difference in the world; this is one of those rare circumstances where you cannot find a lower priced product that has the same craftsmanship and quality as the higher priced one. In the shoe business, craftsmanship and quality take time. And as we all know, time is money, so higher quality shoes will not come cheap.

The main difference is a higher priced shoe will most likely be hand-made, as opposed to machine manufactured for the lower priced. The workmanship for hand-made shoes will be distinct and the color could be hand-finished. For this type of work, you will pay handsomely, for sure. But your feet will thank you later. I don't believe in spending a fortune for a tie because you should have a healthy tie collection, but when it comes to shoes no expense should be spared.

Here are the rules, because everything has rules. Know your feet first. If you take a wide-width shoe, then do not try to squeeze into a narrow European-cut shoe; you will pay in the end from the discomfort. Know your feet well, because once you know the cut you need based on the foot measurements and structure, then you should find the manufacturer that makes shoes that work well with your foot type. You can always search around, like most do, to find a shoe you like that fits, or you can acquaint yourself with a manufacturer that is known for making certain types of shoes that work well with your foot construction. This way, you know in advance the type of cut you will get; regardless of the shoe brand you choose, you should always know the rules

BIG SHOT SHOES!

If you are a fellow who likes to make a statement with handsome shoes, then you may prefer buying footwear in a natural color family such as brown, tan, or cognac. In these colors you will see the detail of the design best; even the texture of the skin will be visible. When it comes to shoes in black, no matter how beautifully designed or skin type, all anyone will see on your feet is a pair of black shoes; unless you are holding them in your hands, the workmanship will be unnoticeable. But, if you like to keep a low profile, you can't go wrong with black shoes. Black shoes are the old standard of conservative dressing, but really do nothing to enhance either your style or the overall presentation of your style. Brown will always do the job, creating a powerful presentation exhibiting the workmanship and details of your shoes. What you should be looking for in a shoe for business and formal occasions is an all-leather construction: the sole should be leather, the outer body should be leather; even the construction of the interior should be leather. From a quality manufacturer this will all be done by hand for the most part.

In the case where your attire is more casual, the choice of shoes with slacks or jeans can be rubber soled; rubber soled shoes are great as an all-weather shoe. Unfortunately, in most cases, you have to sacrifice the stylish looks, because the manufacturer's focus is on the functionality as opposed to design. The thing you must come to grips with is: a shoe is not just a shoe; it is a work of art and truly a labor of love. At the point that you purchase a quality pair of shoes, you will need to maintain them just like you maintain an automobile or anything that needs care. Maintenance includes, but is not limited to, frequent polishing, tap placed on soles, and re-soling annually or as often as needed depending on the frequency of use. It is recommended that you choose among several different pairs of shoes per week, which will prolong the life of each pair and add variation to the look of your wardrobe. You can choose a wide variety of styles and designs: lace-up, slip-on, strapped and two-toned spectator style.

Dress DeCode: 10 Tips Not to Forget

1

A pocket handkerchief adds a dash of flair to a suit, just don't overexpose it.

Brown shoes goes well with both gray and blue suits, save the black shoes for the evening or formal digs.

2

3

A full Windsor knot works only with a cutaway or spread collar shirt.

What really matters is not how wide or narrow a lapel is, but how well it's cut.

4

5

Stay trim so you can wear clothes well. There are also health benefits as well.

Unless you have the artistry of Matisse, only mix patterns in the same color family.

6

7

A tailored vest can add a unique flavor to any suit.

As a general rule, the wider the trouser bottom the wider the cuff, up to the classic 1 ¾ inches.

8

9

A tailored fitted jacket worn with full trouser is preferable to over-sized jacket tight trouser.

Never wear something just because it's trendy. Never!

10

COUNTERPART OF STYLE

"To be trusted is the greatest compliment one can receive"
- Anonymous

"Socks are my absolute favorite accessory; this is an area similar to your tie, where you can let your personality shine through."

Accentuate your life!

The options for choosing the right belt are extensive, but the general rule of thumb when it comes to incorporating your belt into your wardrobe should be that your belt must always be in the same color family as your shoes. In some instances, you can buy the exact matching belt to some pairs of shoes you purchase, but as long as it's in the same color family that will suffice. The great part about identifying the best belts for your wardrobe is to explore all the options; there are many skins, from calf to exotics such as alligator and snakeskin.

You can choose from a wide variety of colors, but keep in mind that in certain instances some skins are better suited than others. I unquestionably encourage you to explore and find the right shoes that compliment your style best, then enhance your look with a belt that works with your shoes.

Socks are my absolute favorite accessory; this is an area similar to your tie, where you can let your personality shine through. Don't hesitate to explore many different colors, textures, and fabrics. I like to look at it this way: no matter how conservative your style may be when you sit down and cross your legs and your socks peek to be exposed, at the very moment a pleasant surprise should ensue.

I like to put a smile on someone's face when they see my socks. This is your opportunity once again to have a conversation piece. A very important point to keep in mind is you do not want your style to be a spectacle; a conversation piece is an entirely different story. You want your style to be admired and appreciated, but certainly not an exhibition where your sense of style or judgment can be questioned. The finished result of developing your own personal style should be to wear clothes well and do it effortlessly; it should be comfortable and you should be at ease.

You can always jazz up your formal, professional, and even casual outfits with a French-cuff shirt, which requires cufflinks. The major rule of thumb when it comes to cufflinks is to find the most unique pair. No two individuals should be wearing the same pair of cufflinks on the same day ever. This is another accessory similar to your hosiery where you should enjoy the practice of searching and finding those one-of-a-kind items. The range of style is truly infinite and the price range is extreme as well; you can purchase a pair of silk-knot cufflinks for $5.00 - $9.00. These are most likely the least expensive pair of decent cufflinks you can buy.

You can also have a custom hand-made pair assembled for you from a company in London; this would cost you anywhere from $600 - $6,000. If you want precious stones to be added, this would account for the higher price. This is certainly an accessory that should always be noticed as an attention-grabber in its very nature or why wear them? They will definitely become a conversation piece, as well they should, and if done correctly you will have a short story to tell about how you came across a small shop with vintage cuff links in Milan and you could not pass up the opportunity to purchase this unique pair of hidden treasures.

A Pocket Rocket

A square for the pocket, better known as a pocket square, is an article of flair that should be used delicately; most men simply put a silk pocket square in their suit breast pocket. But I can assure you that the process is a tad more complicated than that.

There are rules to adhere to when building your self-expressed personal style. Right off the bat, never ever wear a matching tie and pocket square set. I'm not even going to go into detail about why, just remember it's a style taboo.

For someone getting acquainted with his style profile you can start your search yes, this, too, requires a search and find process, the same as with your hosiery and cufflinks. You should be on a continuous hunt for the most unique pocket square you can find.

The proper description is actually a pocket-handkerchief. You don't want it to match your tie exactly, but you do want the tie and handkerchief to have the same principal colors. The actual designs or patterns do not need to be similar because the focus should be the color tones. For the experienced style maven, you are using a different technique. Forget the tie/pocket handkerchief color coordination; your focus will be shirt/pocket handkerchief/sock coordination.

This requires skills that will be developed over time. Your shirt should be in the same color family as the handkerchief, while the handkerchief can have a hint of similar colors as your hosiery as well. This is where you must pay attention to the details and the subtle colors in each piece. To arrive at this level of detail will only come about over time as you build your wardrobe and identify your style comfort level. In time, you will have a healthy handkerchief collection full of colors and designs; you will be able to find the appropriate one for anything you are wearing. So whenever you come across a unique pocket-handkerchief, you should definitely add it to your collection, because it will come in handy some time down the road.

In the mid 80's, braces, better known as suspenders, were all the rage on Wall Street; this was the look of the power brokers. As we moved into the technology and information era, the brick-and-mortar styles of yesteryear went bye-bye. But, it's good to keep in mind that even if a style preference phases out, it doesn't necessarily mean you need to follow suit. Your style should be above the everyday coming and going of fads and phases; your style should be classic at base but contemporary in flair. So, as with braces, this is truly a classic piece, but can remain contemporary by design; there are so many different variations in design, your options will never end. This is really a classic look and should be treated as such, because you need to know when to wear them, and should always wear them with tailored slacks or suit trousers.

The very first bit of information you need to understand about braces is they really do not take the place of a belt. So if you are wearing a pair of trousers that needs a belt, but decide to wear braces, the fit will not be comfortable nor will your look be fitting in the posterior. For the best fit, the trousers need already to be fitted and tailored to your physique; then you add your braces to hold the slacks in place, as well as add a stylish flair to your attire. We are discussing this item from a style perspective, not for those who really need to wear braces because a belt is no longer working for them.

You will need to have your tailor add the button to your trousers or slacks in order to fasten them in place. Once your trousers are fitted with buttons to accommodate your braces, then you can begin your search.

ALWAYS BE ON THE LOOK-OUT!

If you thought your search was over with the pocket-handkerchiefs, you would be wrong; this also requires careful exploration and an exacting taste to find just the right designs to add to your wardrobe. This process should be fun but taken seriously because there are examples of when braces can be taken too far, i.e. Ronald McDonald, Bozo the Clown and affectionately Larry King, so enough said on that topic.

Style Essentials, It's all about the Detail!

SIDEBAR: Having a story to tell can make your entire style experience enjoyable and rewarding, too often in today's fast pace environment people don't take time or the opportunity to have a conversation nor exchange pleasantries as they travel along their journeys each day.

CROWN JEWEL OF STYLE
"Charity covers a multitude of sins, but hats cover more sinners."
(Anonymous)

"For the truly distinguished gentleman, a hat is always an added value complement for Sundays or a special occasion."

KEEP YOUR HEAD UP!

One of my favorite accessories would have to be a well-made hat. The old saying "I'm wearing many hats" rings true; you can truly become whomever you want to be when you wear a hat. It makes you feel with each style of hat you wear as if you're actually living that persona. This distinctive article of clothing can empower any wardrobe. A hat can really take your entire outfit through the roof; it adds that note of sophistication and distinction that only a hat can do.

There is a deep-rooted history of men wearing hats in America, it is said that when John Fitzgerald Kennedy arrived at his Inauguration sans hat, the hat as an everyday tradition went right out the window; some in the media even called him "Hatless Jack" in recognition of President Kennedy's reluctance to wear one. Prior to the 60's demise of the necessity for hats, there was a huge importance for the hat; every man had a collection of hats for every season. Today, a hat can serve as a status symbol, but more importantly it is a symbol of your sense of style.

Return of the Hat!

For the truly distinguished gentleman, a hat is always an added value complement for Sundays or a special occasion. Two of the most popular hats are the fedora and the Panama, but there are many other fashionable hats to wear, so don't be afraid to explore in order to find the best one that suits your face.

Many men no longer wear hats with brims, but choose to don Ivy driver's caps and baseball caps. There is nothing wrong with these hip modern choices of hats, but nothing will ever replace the stylishness of a Panama hat in the summer or a contrast trim felt fedora for the winter or fall. Of course these are known as grown-men's hats, so enough said on that subject.

Stylish Hats

Fedora

Pork Pies

Panama hat

Berets

Driver's cap

Stingy

Newsboy

Homburg

Derby

SIDEBAR: The statement;"I'm wearing many hats" rings true. You can truly become whomever you want to be when you wear a hat, so don't be afraid to be that chap in a hat.

CUSTOMIZATION OF STYLE

"We cannot seek or attain health, wealth, learning, justice or kindness in general. Action is always specific, concrete, individualized and unique."
(John Dewey)

"Regardless of your personality, there are three categories of style that you will fall within."

ACCESSORIZE YOUR LIFE.

The art of style is not found in an expensive suit or sport coat, but the way your attitude and accessories complement the clothes you wear. This is the main ingredient in personal style. The tie you choose says more about your personality than you think. Your watch speaks volumes about the life you lead. Imagine what could be said about a gentleman who chooses not to wear a watch at all.

Here is a crash course on the soul of accessorizing, which is essentially the heart of the anatomy of style. For starters, unless you are the most eccentric cat on the boulevard, don't overdo it. Subtlety is truly the key. The tie enhances the shirt, the sock complements the shoes, and your belt and shoes should be first cousins (in the same color family).

Regardless of your personality, there are three categories of style that you will fall within. Only the most unconventional chap will stand outside the following categories as a true style connoisseur:

DO YOU HAVE STYLE?

The Dapper Don: This guy is always neat and everything is in place. Often wears accessories like a pocket square or cufflinks. He wears his clothes well and with ease.

The Conservative Cat: This guy either doesn't want his clothing to overshadow his ego or doesn't like too much attention. He dresses well and appreciates quality fabrics and tailoring, but will not bother accessorizing his outfit.

The Simple Sam: This guy doesn't know, doesn't show, and downright doesn't care what he wears. He can often be quoted as saying "clothes don't make the man". This poor soul doesn't know any better. His style is not worth mentioning, but often can clean up well with a bit of effort.

If you feel you do not fit into one of the categories, think again. Regardless of your nature, here is the express route to enhancing your wardrobe and supercharging your style without buying a big ticket item like a suit, shoes or overcoat. Let's start from the bottom up.

SIDEBAR: One of the most important style principles you should adopt is the appreciation for a classic style, which will never go out of style.

SOCK IT TO 'EM!

Socks (a.k.a. hosiery in finer men's shops) serve many different purposes, one being to keep the feet warm, so always choose the appropriate thickness in accordance to the weather. The simple rule of thumb (or in this case, big toe) is, your socks should coordinate with either your shoes or trousers, but not both.

Once you understand this basic rule, now you can have fun. Finding unique hosiery should be an ongoing venture, whether traveling or shopping for other garments. Always shop in the hosiery section to find a unique pair that can be added to your current wardrobe. Your socks can easily become a conversation piece and show a different side of your style and personality.

Pick your skin!

A belt also has a very simple rule: it should color-coordinate with your shoes. The beauty of this rule is you can explore many different kinds of skins, from a simple calfskin to an exotic alligator or snake. Once you have chosen the skin you prefer to sport, consider the best place to wear it. Alligator skin, for example, is probably a bit over the top for everyday wear, although some snake skin belts are very fine and can be worn daily with a suit.

A tie varies in size, width, fabric, and patterns so there is no limit to what you can do, but there are rules to this important piece as well. Once you get past some basics, like not pairing stripes with polka dots, or creating dizzying patterns with a vertically striped shirt and horizontal stripes on the tie, now you can have some fun creating your own visual masterpiece.

The new rule of thumb is to let the tie speak for the shirt. So, if you are a modern, stylish fellow who wears patterns and blue shirts as opposed to the basic white collar of days gone by, then you can really explore new ideas and options with your shirt/tie combination. For example, if you have a windowpane shirt in blue with red lines, find a tie that complements the red lines in the shirt, not a tie that matches the blue shirt itself. By accentuating the detail in the shirt, not the shirt itself, your tie will bring out the subtlety of your style. Regardless of the suit color, your shirt and tie should be able to stand alone when you remove your jacket.

Silk scarves and ascots are reserved for the most dapperly of the dapper. This is the one accessory that can single-handedly transform your outfit from informal to formal in a snap. As with your socks, you want to find the most unique silk scarf you can find.

This piece does not need to coordinate with any other garment you are wearing because the entire purpose of the scarf is to stand out. There is a difference between an everyday scarf and one you might wear to a formal event, but you'll be able to discern the difference once you start browsing the men's boutiques.

Dress DeCode: Living Life with Style

1

Invest in Yourself – Growth and development is truly never ending. You should always invest the time to develop yourself. Whether it is furthering your education or strengthening your skills-set; growth and development should be a life-long journey, and you should never hit a final destination. Also, you should also develop your physical being by exercising and staying healthy. We want to be at our best internally and externally.

3

Eat Right – Eating right is one of the key ingredients to fighting diseases. Eating right, staying active and being a non-smoker are the best ways to maintain a healthy life. The key is choosing foods that help maintain a healthy weight. A good diet to try is the Mediterranean diet, which is healthy for your heart.

5

Prioritize – First thing first is the key principle of prioritizing. Group your list of responsibilities and order them in their appropriate importance ranking. In order to accomplish all the things we set out to do in our lives we must first have order. To have order there must be a level of control. Prioritization creates a function of control, which enables us to enjoy the privilege of order. It all sounds so simple; now use it!

2

Breathe Deeply – There are so many benefits to the simple action of breathing deeply, aside from the obvious breath-of-life. Taking a moment out of each day to breathe deeply has many health benefits. The immediate benefit of a deep breathing exercise is stress relief and detoxification of carbon dioxides. Go on and take your minute to breathe deeply and de-stress.

4

Meditate – Meditation is a way to bring your body to a peaceful rest. It does not matter how you choose to practice meditation; all that really matters is you must engage in thoughts, contemplation or moments of reflection. It can also be spiritual introspection. Meditation if practiced regularly can bring a level of peace to your life that we all so desperately need.

Exercise – It seems exercise is always promoted for its muscle and strength benefits when it comes to men. There is nothing wrong with being a muscle man if that is what you want to be. But, I encourage everyone to seriously focus on the health benefits of daily exercise. The merit of daily exercise range from improvement in mood swings to the prevention of chronic health conditions. The overall benefits of daily exercising can be the difference between life and; should I say it? Stay healthy!

Eat Light – We all need to eat; some of us love to eat. I often proclaim that I eat to live and do not live to eat. A Mediterranean diet provides an ideal diet that is healthy for the heart. This diet incorporates the basic healthy menu with the benefits of lots of fruit and the privilege of a glass of wines with your meal. Research has shown the health benefit of the Mediterranean diet is off the charts. So, as you shoot for the sky, do not forget to eat right and eat light.

Love – There are certainly great health and life extending benefits to having love in your life. Whether you are married or have a loved one, as long as you have love in your life researcher have shown wide-ranging benefits like; lower cholesterol, strengthening of immune system, lower blood pressure and long extended love can even result in living life longer. Who knew having love in your heart was so good for your heart?

Travel – I mention a host of benefits from being well traveled in the World of your Style section of this book, but there are many more benefits to being a world traveler. We often identify a renaissance man as someone with a broad perspective, wide experience and well traveled. The added benefit of traveling is meeting new people; seeing many places and experiencing many difference cultures. Once you see the world you will really feel a part of the world.

Appreciate – Having the ability to appreciate all things, whether large or small is the same as giving thanks. We should always take a moment to give thanks for our mere existence, but don't stop there. Look around you and show appreciation for the ones you love, for the things you have, and for the life you live. When one takes time to appreciate, this exemplifies a level of responsibility for what you have, and a tell-tale sign you are ready for more.

TIMEKEEPER OF STYLE

"Dost thou love life? Then do not squander time; for that's the stuff life is made of."
(Benjamin Franklin)

"A timepiece is much more than just a timekeeper. It's a tool that marks the moments and days of your life."

A timepiece is much more than just a timekeeper. It's a tool that marks the moments and days of your life. For some people this notion may be a bit extreme, but you have no idea how the watch you wear speaks volumes about you and your lifestyle. The choice in style, size and even brand can clarify certain details about the life you lead. What does your timepiece say about you?

Let's say hypothetically, you are working as a hedge fund manager for a Wall Street financial firm and you walk in on Monday morning with a super-sized, blinged-out, diamond-encrusted watch on that could be spotted from a mile away. What message would that particular timepiece say about you; what message would it convey to your colleagues and clients? To most people in that environment, it would scream lapses in judgment. More importantly, in a position where sound judgment is your business it wouldn't be wise, unless you own the joint, in that case bling-on! For the rest of us, let's send the right message while keeping the right time and being on time.

SIDEBAR: For the true man of style, nothing beats the classic, nostalgic look of a pocket watch. There are so many designs and styles of pocket watches to choose from. When you come out of your pocket with this bad boy the world will know that time is on your side. Literally!

Atomic time!

The first thing we should understand about a timepiece is that the time should be accurate. The U.S. NAVY keeps an official time called the Atomic Time, this is the most precise time, even news and media outlets set their programming from the Atomic Time. The reason I'm pointing this out is because there are two types of timepieces you can own: quartz or an automatic movement. A quartz movement is controlled by a little battery that should be changed annually. An automatic movement is controlled by the movement of your wrist; every time you move your wrist it winds your watch. The automatic movement is the oldest form, dating back hundreds of years. The craft of designing this type of movement is still an old world art that has become synonymous with Switzerland and their timepiece expertise. The quartz movement is usually less expensive and some have argued that it provides a more accurate movement because it is controlled by a battery. As long as the battery has full strength, the time will always be accurate where as the automatic movement will lose time if your timepiece rests for too long a period of time. For most of the more reputable brands, the reserve period can be as much as two to three days. One thing is guaranteed is this: if you leave an automatic watch in a resting mode for more than a week, your watch will need to be readjusted and reset.

Now that we had a crash course in the movement of timepieces, now we can find what works best for you. Let's throw out the cost factor. A timepiece can cost anything from a New York City "Canal Street $10 special" to a high-end piece costing $100,000.00 from a fine retailer. What kind of watch best suits your lifestyle? You may find that given your life, you may need to own a couple of timepieces, one for work and one for more social/casual events. You may even have a collection of watches for different occasions; this wouldn't qualify you as a collector, but rather, someone who understands that in everything you do there are different tools required.

Back to the Wall Street hedge fund manager with the lapse in judgment—if you decide to acquire a precious stone-clad timepiece which can be very expensive, you are in luck because there are many brands that design this style. It will only be a matter of how much you are willing to spend. Just keep in mind that going to the supermarket with this piece won't get you a discount on your sirloin, but at the local bar, anything is possible.

For the gentleman who is more active or wants to make a bold statement, you can wear a full-size stainless steel piece, which comes in a wide variety of dial colors from an even wider range of makers. This style is probably the most popular for a man especially in America.

For the chap who likes to be more refined and stylish, he might prefer a leather strap piece. Most straps are interchangeable so you can always replace the strap with a different style or color, based on whatever your heart desires.

For the true man of style, nothing beats the classic, nostalgic look of a pocket watch. There are so many designs and style of pocket watches to choose from. When you come out of your pocket with this bad boy the world will know that time is on your side.

WHAT TIME IS IT?

In this fast-paced technologically controlled environment we live in, everything is constrained by time, whether it is our computer, PDA, or MP3 player, but I think there is no excuse for walking around without some form of timepiece. The statement about who you are and what you are about when you do not wear a watch is that time is not of importance to you and having that knowledge is insignificant to you.

Now that you have read this, toss your "Canal Street $10 special" for a better quality timekeeper, the perfect one that encapsulates who you are and what you stand for. Tell the world who you really are, you will be proud to say that you finally know what time it is.

CASUALTY OF STYLE

"Do not fear mistakes, there are none."
- Miles Davis

"Let's face it: being a man of style or being revered for your stylish aptitude is not for everybody."

Don't Let Your Style be a Casualty!

I know this book focused a good amount of time on suits and ties, and I'm sure everyone does not wear suits and ties all the time, let alone every day. I know many men prefer to be comfortable, and for some men casual comfort is more important than how you look. Those men assume that dressing less, while looking casual and comfortable, is their way of expressing themselves. But if you learned anything from this book, you should know by now if the fit is right and your **Style DNA**™ has been identified you will be comfortable in anything you are wearing.

What you need to keep in mind is your casual collection is already in your closet, you just need to know how to pull out different pieces to create a casual style that will not detract from your overall style. Remember your sport coat is the most dependable article of clothing you have in your wardrobe; you can wear it to the office and pull together a casual look for the sports bar as well. Remember that it's okay to have a comfortable laidback, casual style, but there's an art to it; just like any other style, there are things you should wear and there are things you should never wear. You want your casual style to be transitional to the point where you will be able to glide through different scenes and still look like you are dressed aptly. You should always play it cautiously when it comes to being casual, because you never know where the day is going to take you.

For those who enjoy the variety that life has to offer, let's talk about casual wear and the best way to pull off this look without damaging your style repertoire.

WHAT YOU SHOULD HAVE IN YOUR CASUAL COLLECTION:

- Blazer

- Sweater

- Fitted T-Shirt

- Jeans

- Brown Shoes (*remember the black shoes rule, formal and funerals only*)

- Slim cut track suit (*being in shape is important for this one or you'll look like a made man*)

- Hat collection (*yes, it can include caps of your favorite teams*)

WHAT YOU SHOULD NOT HAVE IN YOUR CASUAL COLLECTION:

- Oversized sport jersey

- Oversized T-Shirt

- Baggy Jeans

- Work Boots (*unless you are hiking or a lumberjack*)

- Anything from your college or high school days

IT'S YOUR STYLE!

Let's face it: being a man of style or being revered for your stylish aptitude is not for everybody. You are going to have to be a chap who truly wants to stand alone and let the world know that what you wear is your style and cannot be duplicated or mass-produced. The way you carry yourself and your attitude must be on point to solidify the overall effect. At the end of the day, taking into account the benefits of having a smart/casual look vs. the distraction of having a sloppy, sleep-in look, you decide what perception you want to convey with your laidback style.

Here is a true trade secret that should be applied to your casual collection. If you are one of those dudes who values your casual style and chooses to reject all conventional wisdom bestowed upon you through this book, here are some tips that will instantly enhance the casual/comfortable style that you desperately hold on to. You can accessorize your casual style with sunglasses, shoes and hats. Regardless of what you are wearing, adding just one of these style enhancers can turn your jeans and T-shirt into an eclectic look that will become uniquely your style. Let's say you are a jeans and T-shirt chap and enjoy this relaxed look over and above others. If you add an awesome pair of sunglasses or tinted lens glasses for indoor use, this will instantly transform your look from comfort to cool. The enhancement will be noticeable immediately; those outstanding opticals will become the focal point, forcing people to focus more on your face.

As I mentioned in an earlier chapter the paramount importance of having well-made shoes. Well, in this instance, maybe this is the best example I can provide. Because no matter how casual your style may be, with a pair of well-made hard-soled shoes, you will be displaying to the world a little taste of the possibilities of your style. This will be a small gesture proclaiming I could dress well if I wanted to, but choose to have a more relaxed look, notwithstanding the appreciation for quality. Now, I know you are saying to yourself, "having on well-made shoes will communicate all that?" in fact, having on well-made shoes speaks louder than having on a $5,000 suit. Choosing exceptional footwear and mixing it with your casual style will speak volumes to your inherent style taste. Try it, you'll see! Then you can thank me later.

Casual Cool!

The ultimate casual style enhancer is a hat. As I covered in a previous section of this book, wearing many hats has different effects. So a hat can always take an outfit to the next level, and your casual look is no exception to this rule. If you are leisurely running some errands over the weekend you can put on a blazer, shirt and jeans, but if you add a hat like a Porkpie, Straw fedora, Ivy Driver's cap, or French beret, this will create an instant eye-catcher, which will boost your style points exponentially.

You see, adding style enhancers create an organic look that cannot be duplicated, although others will try. This speaks to paying attention to the details; you can never go wrong with accents that contrast the overall look, while often times becoming the focal point of your look. The first thing people will notice is the funky hat, or the oversized aviator optical, and at end of the day you can still have the relaxed look that you had all along, but jazzed up with a little personal flair.

WORLD OF STYLE

"When you do the common things in life in an uncommon way, you will command the attention of the world."
- George Washington Carver

"Just like you would map out a travel route before taking a long driving trip, you need to map out your dress route as well."

ARE YOU READY FOR THE WORLD?

How do your style and your appearances affect the world in which you live? Moreover, how does the world in which you live affect your style? If you are going to be a man of style, it makes no sense to be recognized as a stylish gentleman when you are in your home country, but have your style fall short when you travel the world. Before you grab your passport and make any travel arrangements, you need to know the style customs of your travel destinations. Many places around the world have certain particular customs and inherent style traits.

I can't stress enough how important it is to know these customs and traits before you enter a foreign destination, since overlooking or just plain ignoring the mores of many places throughout the world could be viewed as disrespectful. On the other hand, if you get off the plane in traditional garbs that are designated to locals, which may symbolize an important cultural value, in some places this can be deemed disrespectful as well. Yes, it's the good ole Catch-22 scenario.

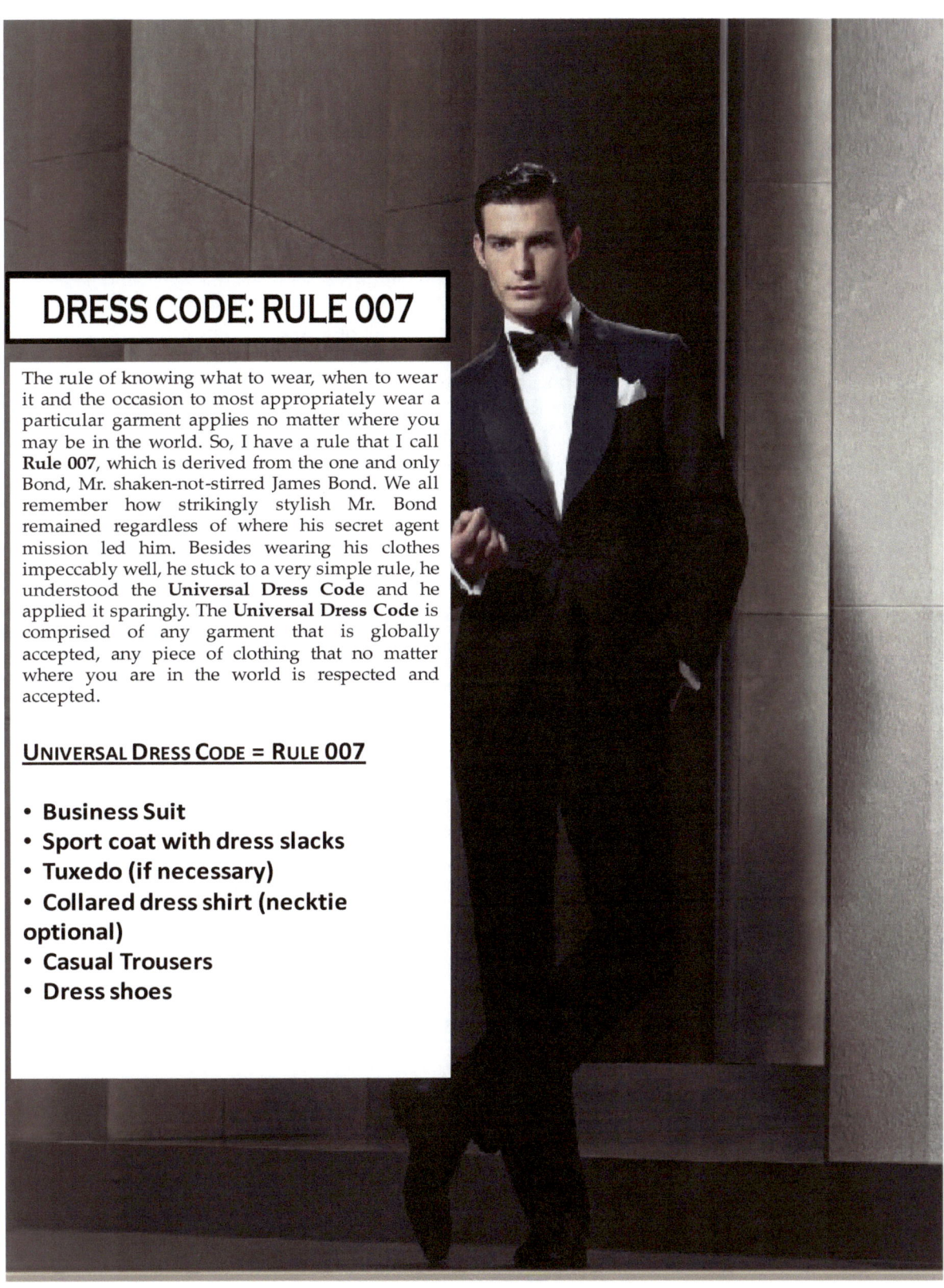

DRESS CODE: RULE 007

The rule of knowing what to wear, when to wear it and the occasion to most appropriately wear a particular garment applies no matter where you may be in the world. So, I have a rule that I call **Rule 007**, which is derived from the one and only Bond, Mr. shaken-not-stirred James Bond. We all remember how strikingly stylish Mr. Bond remained regardless of where his secret agent mission led him. Besides wearing his clothes impeccably well, he stuck to a very simple rule, he understood the **Universal Dress Code** and he applied it sparingly. The **Universal Dress Code** is comprised of any garment that is globally accepted, any piece of clothing that no matter where you are in the world is respected and accepted.

UNIVERSAL DRESS CODE = RULE 007

- **Business Suit**
- **Sport coat with dress slacks**
- **Tuxedo (if necessary)**
- **Collared dress shirt (necktie optional)**
- **Casual Trousers**
- **Dress shoes**

Travel essential tools!

You should always travel with garments that are universally accepted as formal and informal wear; whether you are traveling for business or pleasure, dressing for the occasion enhances the entire experience. The first thing we want to focus on is traveling light, only packing things that you are actually going to use. You can accomplish this by mapping out your itinerary and researching the dress requirements for all activities you plan on enjoying, whether it's clear or unstated. No matter where you are, every place has a dress requirement. Have you ever attended an event and felt under- or over-dressed? That's because you did not map out your dress route in advance.

You should always check the dress requirements before attending any event. There are several benefits to doing so. One, you will be appropriately dressed for each occasion; two, you won't find yourself making this careless wardrobe misstep, which can result in you having unexpectedly to purchase something suitable to wear; and third, it can be much too costly to replace a wardrobe while traveling.

MAP YOUR DRESS ROUTE!

Just like you would map out a travel route before taking a long driving trip, you need to map out your dress route as well. You should know the clothing requirements before going anywhere; this may include calling ahead and asking the dress code or asking someone who has been to a particular place before. If the occasion is important, like a first date or entertaining a business client, passing by the location days ahead of your scheduled date may be necessary as well. The worst unprepared act you can be guilty of, besides not having enough money to pay for an evening you are the host of, is not being dressed appropriately for the occasion. This act is taboo and must be avoided at all cost.

While traveling in another country, if all fails your point of reference for dress requirements, queries should be directed to the hotel concierge. The concierge will be able to help with the conundrum of matters related to proper dress and, if he does not have the answer offhand, he will be happy to make the necessary calls to find out this precious information for you. Just one thing you must remember: tip the concierge well; you never know when his or her services will be needed again.

You may ask yourself what is the importance of understanding the **Universal Dress Code**? Well, there are several benefits, the primary one being the respect dressing appropriately commands. While traveling, you do not want to look like a tourist who is seeking a good time because you will become a mark, and I'm not even going to get into what happens to a mark in foreign lands. The look you are seeking is casual-smart with a clean look that communicates you enjoy life and take pleasure in nice things, because this is how you will be treated when shopping, dining or sightseeing. Some restaurants have collard-shirt or jacket required dress codes, and although they will lend you a jacket if you come ill-prepared, you may find yourself enjoying dinner in one two sizes too big and looking ridiculous, which could ruin what might otherwise have been a perfect experience. Always ask dress requirements when making your reservation, if you are unsure. Do not take this for granted.

Be Ready For Anything!

The additional benefit of dressing well while traveling will be clear if your destination is Europe or Asia in particular, because in these regions of the world people generally dress very well. They tend to dress well for work and leisure alike. So, if you are thinking about packing your jeans and T-shirt collection, think again and save that for lounging around your hotel room.

The one thing you should understand is in Europe and Asia your appearance is serious business. There are many stories about American tourists being at the receiving end of ill-treatment in places like Hong Kong and Paris because their appearance was not refined enough. Some may see this as snobbish behavior, but clearly this behavior is not just for the sake of being snobbish. In fact, these are very old nations with rich traditions that seem to work very hard at maintaining them. So it would be a huge mistake to think that you're going to bring your laid-back comfort/casual sense of style to these locales and be pleasantly welcomed; if so, you are in for a rude awakening, no pun intended.

Other appearance-conscious cities include Milan, Japan, London, Spain, and the list goes on. I suggest you bring you're A-game when it comes to dressing while traveling and be willing to learn a thing or two. Each city and every culture has a bit of style and substance you can take away and incorporate these elements into your own wardrobe, and return home a little more stylish and a lot more cultured.

Globetrotting in Style

Here is one fact that rings true whether you are trekking around the world or staying home: being well dressed will give you access to many places and state of affairs while garnering treatment that is welcoming no matter where you may be. We live in a world where enjoying life and living well is much to be desired; people want to live well whether they can afford it or not. It's true that many civil societies with a high standard of living have a great regard for their quality-of-life and comfortably enjoy a clean environment. Among the many advantages they benefit from are low crime rates, low poverty levels, low homelessness rate and a high morale for their outlook on life in the future. These societies also enjoyed dressing well and have an expectation that everyone shares this standard, sound too good to be true? Well, the top ten nations with the highest standard of living enjoy these advantages, which include the tendency of being neatly attired. There is certainly a correlation between high standards of living and the tendency to dress presentably, because this seems to be a trait of nations with the highest standards. There is much to be said for having a presentable appearance and how it affects the world around you.

77

PSYCHOLOGY OF STYLE
"Knowledge speaks, but wisdom listens."
- Jimi Hendrix

"The very first element of making an impression on yourself is being true to thyself."

How do you feel?

Most people would not automatically associate what you wear with psychology or your emotions. In fact, you would probably associate social economics with what you wear before psycho-emotions. But the way you think about yourself, your world, including the feeling derived from your overall views, have significant impact on how you choose to dress. There have been numerous studies done on this topic, countless papers written about the psychology of clothes.

In the studies, you can find a wide range of views about people's idiosyncrasies on why they will do what they do or choose to wear what they wear. I'm not about to go into deep science about neuro-kinetics, brain waves or emotional connections and how they may have played a part in the last article of clothing you purchased. But, I will confirm that your thoughts and emotions subconsciously dictate your choices when it comes to your appearance. But what I want to examine even more is how what you choose to wear influences how you are feeling.

There is definitely a direct correlation between how you look and how you feel; this is another principle that can be turned into practice simply by getting up in the morning and putting on a new outfit, which can give you thoughts and feelings of optimism for that day; your outlooks for that day can be positive, allowing your appearance to be empowering and encouraging wishful thinking. This can happen without you even being aware of the psycho-emotions that are in full effect. Although this is not a new discovery, unfortunately, we more often see this play itself out in a negative manner.

We have all seen someone we know was in a funk; they don't want to be bothered and find themselves lying around in the old sweatshirt or housecoat. They can't hold themselves together enough to fix their hair or make up their face. The feeling that a person is experiencing at that moment is clearly controlling the fact that they have no desire to spruce themselves up, and this would be the common scenario when someone is feeling down.

I'm sure when you are in a funk; you have little or no desires to put on anything spectacular. But what if putting on something spectacular was just the cure you needed to make yourself feel better under those circumstances when you feel anything but spectacular? Would you do it?

How is your spirit?

Let's take this a little further and see just how what you are wearing can control how you are feeling. The way to best apply this ideology is to have it work in a positive manner for you. We discussed being approachable and leaving a positive impression on others, but now we must focus on the impression you leave on yourself. Yes, you heard correctly. What type of impression do you leave on yourself?

Let's face it, if you can't impress yourself, how in the world do you expect to make a powerful impression on someone else? The very first element of making an impression on yourself is being true to thyself. Yes, I know it sounds Biblical, but actually it's spiritual. Before you can make a positive impression on the world around you, the world within you must get in sync. You need to allow your inner self to commune with your outer self, which will then enable you freely and comfortably to express yourself.

When you get to this point, there is no one who can stop you. You will become a force of nature that will be a breath of fresh air to all who come into your presence. I know it sounds like a York Peppermint Patty commercial, but the effect you can have on others is real.

Before you get nervous and assume that I'm going to urge you to run to church, I want to be clear, I said this process is not Biblical, it's spiritual. So you must allow your innermost attributes to shine through; this includes your attitude, your outlook and, of course, your personality.

When you change the way you think, you can change the way you feel. Some skeptics might feel it's only clothes and should not be anything more than that. You will find those skeptics who will say things like "clothes don't make the man". You can also say a book is only words, or in some cases pictures, but the fact is what you think about something is not what's most important; as with clothes or books it's what you take away that is most important. The effect of the cause is what's going to bring you the most beneficial results.

Remember, we are talking about how your appearance can be a contributing factor to you being a better you. I can agree with the statement that clothes don't make the man, but clothes can certainly make the man look and feel better.

You Must Look Into the mirror!

So let me clearly bring my theory of psycho-emotion and the role it all plays in making a powerful impression together. I spoke of each individual creating his own **Style DNA™**; this is a process that must start from within. All of your hopes, desires, dreams and aspirations will be the main ingredients of the recipe of this process. Most people walk around and in most cases, regardless of what they are wearing, it doesn't truly reflect who they really are. They go about their lives with a costume masking the real person undoubtedly lying within. You can start by asking yourself, what do I want the world to know about me, how do I want the world to feel about me? Yes, the world; we can't think small in a narrow scope like the only thing that matters is the little environment in which we live. For you to be successful in creating the powerful image you should be reaching for, you must have a global perspective with a sprinkle of a worldview on top. You must understand that being versatile and agile is the spice that you will need to add to the main ingredients, which will help you complete the **Style DNA™** discovery process.

STYLE DNA SELF-CONCEPT PROCESS

- How do you feel about yourself?

- How accurate are those feelings?

- What do you want the world to know about you?

- How do you want the world to feel about you?

- What do I feel comfortable wearing on a daily basis?

- What colors makes me feel excited?

- If you met yourself for the first time today, what would you think about you?

- Walking out of the house every day, are you truly happy with your appearance?

- If money was not an issue, what would you wear each day?

- Do you think your loved ones and friends are proud to walk down the street with you based on your appearance?

- If so, why?

- If not, why?

You Must Look Within!

When you honestly ask yourself these questions and truly answer them without any reservations as to the outcome of the responses, then you can begin to build your personal style. Having the willingness to celebrate your strengths and the courage to understand your weaknesses will allow you the opportunity to usher in the growth you need to complete the anatomy of your style.

This self reflecting process will open the opportunity to explosive results that will stay with you for a lifetime, allowing you to create the style that can best represent who you are in your entirety and promote the many facets of your personality. I hope at this point there are no remaining non-believers who don't fully understand the essential need of developing a personal style, which will allow you to be a better you. If you read this book up to this point, it's safe to assume that you got it and you are now prepared to run with it.

All in all, the one thing I want you to remember about the psychology of your style is that dressing your best and putting your best foot forward at all times, for any occasion, not only can be the extra tool you need to accentuate your positives, but it can also add as an emotional boost in the moments when you are feeling uncertain or unmotivated. Just get up and put on something fresh and clean. You will see from one positive reaction to another, you will feel your confidence level building like a rocket booster raring to blast off. And if all else fails, at least you'll look sharp-- and that can't be all that bad, right?

VOICE OF STYLE

"The most important thing in communication is to hear what isn't being said."
- Peter Drucker

"We have all heard the old wives' tale about how the size of your shoes matters, but in reality how well you maintain your shoes matters even more."

Does size matter?

What is your appearance saying about you? This is a thought provoking question that all men should ask themselves at one point or another. Because regardless of who you are or what's your style, your appearance is most definitely communicating something about you.

There are those who are well aware of this, but, on the other hand, there are those who most certainly are not. For the ones who remain unaware, this chapter is for you.

We have all heard the old wives' tale about how the size of your shoes matters, but in reality how well you maintain your shoes matters even more. Because when someone looks down at a well-shined shoe, what that communicates is, I am a person who pays attention to details.

Now this does not mean that if you choose to sport scruffy shoes that you're not a person who pays attention to details, but with well-shined shoes on your feet, the message will certainly be clear.

Although I'm using your shoes as an illustration, this applies to everything that you wear. So just like you may ask yourself, or someone else, do I look good in this suit, shirt or sweater, you also need to go further and develop the courage to ask yourself, what is what I'm wearing saying about me?

It's easy to overlook this important self-examination process, just as it is simple to take the easy way out by ignoring what others may think about you; to not care takes no effort at all. And if you lived on an island somewhere far out in the Pacific, this notion would be perfectly fine and I would agree. But you don't, so start your **Style DNA**™ process and go through the rigorous practice of determining if what you're wearing is communicating the message you would like to send to the world.

We all must be responsible for our own actions, we must take responsibility for all the things that we do, but in most cases taking responsibility is neither easy nor simple. Therefore, if you work in an environment that allows business casual or a relaxed dress atmosphere, even if this may be the policy of your business, it doesn't necessarily mean that this business casual policy should govern your wardrobe.

ALWAYS BE READY!

You must always use your best judgment when it comes to determining what you should wear for any given occasion. Believe it or not, what you choose to wear on any given day will have a great impact on the response others give to you throughout that day. This is a fact that can be turned into an exercise. You can get up in the morning one day and try this out for yourself. Put on a tracksuit and a comfortable pair of sneakers and go do your daily routine, whether it's during the week or on the weekend.

Now, allow a few days to go by, and put on a suit or a blazer with slacks you can even put on a blazer with jeans-- and go through the same exact routine you did with the tracksuit, and I guarantee you the actions and responses that you will get from people will be extremely different, even if it is from the same individuals.

No one should accept this fact, nor take this reality, lightly; you want to turn this exercise into a tool that you can use for your own benefit.

If you ever wondered what type of reception would you receive before you went out, the fact is, this can be determined even before you get out of bed by merely making the right or wrong choice when choosing what you going to wear that day.

In earlier chapters I clearly defined the benefits of standing out in a crowd, but when I say stand out, of course I mean it in a positive way, not in a damaging manner. Therefore, you must examine your environment and understand what the acceptable dress code is.

After you determine the acceptable dress code, you will want to one-up it, don't be afraid to take it to the next level. It's okay to dress a little better then the people around you, it's okay to send a clear message that how I look matters to me. Just so as long as what you are wearing is sending a positive message about who you are and what you stand for and that message should communicate excellence.

Dress the part!

It all comes down to the boundless desire to be successful; therefore, dressing in the manner that sends a positive message at all times is an absolute must. You never know what opportunities can arise from maximizing your appearance. I am a staunch believer that you should be ready at all times for successful opportunities. There is an old saying, opportunities knock lightly; not only is this true, but opportunities also come around when least expected. A great opportunity is not going to wait until you go home and find the appropriate things to wear, and then upon your return, allow you to take your rightful place as the beneficiary of the opportunity. I can assure you this is not going to happen. You must be ready, willing and able at any given time to embrace opportunities when they present themselves. What you wear should reinforce the notion that I am ready, I am the person for the opportunity and I can get the job done.

DRESS FOR THE OCCASION!

Most people take for granted the art of dressing for the occasion, whether it's for the job or even a social event. Dressing for the occasion plays a major role in the overall experience. When you put on your suit and tie, add your cufflinks and well-shined shoes, nothing can ruin your outlook for that day; and this is the way it should be.

When you dress well, you feel like there's nothing you can't accomplish. Your overall approach will greatly be affected by what you wear. It's like a tennis match where you hit the ball to one player and that player hits the ball back, and the ball goes back and forth.

It's the same thing when it comes to dressing well in your business environment, you get a positive reaction from being well dressed, and that positive feedback is encouragement that will fuel the fire for your doing well, or at least it should. This is something that just doesn't serve you well in a work setting, but also works well in any surrounding.

WORLD-CLASS STYLE!

When you are working within environments where everything is in its place, and everyone is represented professionally, this is the type of environment that cultivates productivity. If you went around the world to the most respected and successful companies, the first thing you would notice most is a professionally represented environment. This is not even an option, this is the rule. But if you don't have the good fortune to work in one of these world-class companies, it doesn't mean you can't approach your work in a world-class manner. It all starts with dressing for the occasion; if you want to be successful this cannot be overlooked.

If you are an individual who is constantly seeking to improve yourself, then I'm sure you have read many books about how to get ahead in business. One common denominator I find among these self-help manuals is that they encourage individuals not to out-dress the boss. Here and there, you may find a book that will say things like "do not dress for the job you have, but for the job you want". I rebuff both pieces of advice. I believe once you have established your style, this will carry you through as you ascend to the pinnacle of your profession.

You definitely want to survey the environment where you work; you must be aware of how well your coworkers pay attention to the dress policies. In any office, you will have those who dress very professionally, and then you will have those individuals who can be looked upon as slackers who will choose to wear just about anything and have clearly put little thought into their appearance. To be the best, you want to build a reputation for delivering quality work. At the same time, you want to have a reputation for a quality presentation. You want your presentation and work reputation to be so highly regarded that if a new project or opportunity were to arise, your name would be at the top of the list.

Building a highly regarded appearance takes time, so consistency is the key here. I also encourage you to try a wide array of styles over a period of time. Every now and then, you can break away from the suit and tie and try a cardigan sweater, a cardigan vest or add a vest to your suit. I recommend trying something different once or twice a week; this will allow you to keep your image fresh and appear to have an expanded wardrobe even if you don't.

DRESS YOURSELF!

When I speak to the voice of your style, it's important to bear in mind that if you don't dress yourself then it's not your voice. I know a lot of men don't have the patience to shop around and others don't possess the taste or know-how to find the right things to wear, so you relegate this task to your wife, girlfriend, significant other, or momma. You have to dress yourselves, Gentlemen! It's the only way your inner voice will shine brightly through, which will allow all the wonderful aspects of you to be meticulously woven within your entire presentation. If someone else is shopping for you or picking out your clothes then the voice of your style is not your voice. When you select each and every detail of what you wear the very fabric of what makes you who you are shines through. Additionally, there is an emotional connection as it relates to your style having a voice; the connection is with those closest to you.

I was recently watching a lifestyle show on one of those cable networks. In this segment of the show, the host was interviewing a woman who was commenting about her husband's style, or lack thereof. The woman kept telling the host about the days when she first met her husband prior to their careers and children. He used to dress so well and always had a well put-together appearance. She smiled as she reflected upon those happy beginnings. She went on to speak about their current routines and told the story with a bit of frustration and pain about her yearnings for days gone by.

She recalled the days when they used to dress up and go out; they would have so many fun-filled times. She clearly took pleasure in talking about the moments when enjoyable times were had by all. Of course, after having children, their priorities took a 180-degree turn and now the children were their main focus.

At this point the host spoke to the husband, who surely recognized that he no longer had the time nor desire to dress well. He said that as a carpenter in the theater district, there was no need to put on anything decent to perform his job. So, the ripped-up jeans and T-shirt not only became his work attire, but it became his wardrobe. To his wife's dismay he wore his jeans and T-shirt all the time, regardless of where they would go. It became clear to me that this was one of those makeover shows, and, unbeknownst to the husband, he was about to be given a new look.

SPEAK WITHOUT SAYING A WORD!

Based on my observation of the wife's frustration and discontent with her husband's current appearance, I was looking forward to the husband's makeover, at least for the wife's sake. At this point we can all guess how it ended: the husband was made over and he looked completely different (in a good way) and the wife was tearfully overjoyed and everyone lived happily ever after. What struck a chord in me about this show was the wife's desire to have her husband back looking the way she remembered him when they first met . . . and how much it meant to her to once again experience the feelings of those enjoyable moments she felt they had lost.

This is a perfect example of how what you wear and what you do can have a tremendous impact on those around you. It doesn't have to be a loved one, it can be a boss who would like you to attend a meeting with potential new clients, but feels your appearance is not up to snuff and, unbeknownst to you, chooses not to invite you. How you look sends a clear message to others, how it's received can have an emotional effect on others without you even knowing.

On the other hand, if you work in a more casual environment, to establish a style that will be highly regarded and respected, I recommend not wearing khakis pants or a polo shirt, not even on Fridays. What you want to wear is comfortable slacks, which come in a wide variety of shades and fabrics. Additionally, always wear a buttoned-down shirt, and make sure it is always pressed.

if you just focus on slacks and a buttoned-down shirt, that combination alone has enormous possibilities. There are so many designs and colors you can find in a buttoned-down shirt; you can have French cuff or button cuff. And when it comes to slacks, you can have many shades and textures, flannel or tweed. And in the summer months, don't be shy about pulling out the linen pants. If you accessorize this combination well, with the right shoes and belts, in a casual environment you will look like you are ready for anything.

A JACKET IS THE TOTAL PACKAGE!

One of the best pieces of clothing you can have in your wardrobe is a sports coat; it provides multiple levels of versatility. This will end up being the single most important piece in your wardrobe, because of its anytime, anyplace, anywhere versatility. As with your slacks, a sports coat comes in a wide variety of fabric textures and shades. But the rules for your sports coat are very different from your slacks. You want to make sure that you stick to dark colors and subtle texture. You don't want your sports coat to be making any big statements with bold colors for one very important reason; you want to be able to wear it time and time again without being noticeable to everyone. A sports coat can become one of those can't live without pieces of clothing once you find the right fit in the right fabric, you will wear it so often that they will have to pry it off your back.

      A sports jacket is the one garment that you can wear every day with other pieces of clothing. As long as you have a freshly pressed shirt and neatly pressed slacks, you can wear your seasonal sports coat every day. Because a sports coat is so versatile, again this is the one article of clothing that can even float into the weekend. You can grab your sports jacket with a polo shirt and a pair of jeans and go about your leisurely activities on your days off. You can pair your sports jacket with just about anything. You can wear a cardigan under it or you can wear a shirt and tie. This is the perfect tool if you work in a casual environment because there will never be a need to wear a suit at all.

You Got The Look!

I'm going to provide you with some great examples of what a smart style should look like, I recommend you try some of these combinations and see how these smart styles work for you. No matter what your position is within any organization, you cannot go wrong if you have a smart style; if you are striving for excellence within the position you hold, a smart style will communicate excellence without saying a word.

If you are a person who has a limited wardrobe and don't have many sport jackets in your closet to spool through many different looks, here is your best bet; if working in a business casual environment I recommend you wear your business suits every day with a buttoned-down shirt excluding a tie. This is the best way to position yourself to be ready for anything. It's one thing to dress business casual while you're working, but what if something else might arise during the course of the day that requires a suit and tie? If you follow my suggestion, the only thing you would be missing is a tie.

I had such an experience some years ago. I was consulting with a company that had a suit but no tie is necessary policy. Late in the afternoon, one of the managing directors asked me to accompany him to a client's event, which was taking place that evening. Of course I knew that a jacket and tie were required for this event. I simply ran out and purchased a tie. I did so because I knew this type of circumstance would not happen every day. Once I added my new tie to the suit I was wearing, who outside the office would have known that we worked in a business casual environment? Now if you take that same scenario, but I was wearing a pair of khakis, a polo shirt or even a buttoned-down shirt, there would have been no way I could have transformed what I was wearing into the dress appropriate for that evening event. You see, it's in your best interests to always position yourself where you are prepared for anything that should arise.

Look smart!

LEADING THE PACK!

If you chose to wear a suit with a buttoned-down shirt in your business casual environment, this combination has the same versatility as with your sports jacket. Once you are in the office, you will remove your suit jacket and for the duration of the day and you will be functioning in your slacks and a buttoned-down shirt. Wearing your suit without a tie allows you to really explore many options in shirts, patterns and colors. Under these circumstances I would encourage wearing a marvelous patterned shirt that stands out and makes a statement. Keep in mind that once you remove your suit jacket, your shirt is where everyone's attention will be focused. So it doesn't hurt to give them something good to look at.

We know that everyone does not set out with a dress to impress philosophy. And that's fine, because it is big world we live in, and everyone is not successful nor strives to be.

So the fact is, you may get some grief from your colleagues and co-workers. Someone may ask why you dress the way you do, which should clearly exceeds the company's policy. My suggestion is to ignore everyone who doesn't understand your method, because your style, as with your reputation, will be established over time, and in due course all those questions will be satisfied. It's easy to get trapped in a box and feel like, when you are within a certain environment or the workplace, you must fit in as opposed to standing out. And this may be true if you want to be looked upon as one of the crowd. But if you are planning on being at the head of the pack, then fitting in is not your goal. Your mission is to become the new establishment. You want to raise the bar and enhance your environment, as a leader should. Standing out is a method you want to embrace if your plans are to be a success.

If being at the center of attention is not for you, it is understandable, this methodology may take some time to get used to and be effectively applied. But at the point you are chosen to lead the pack you must be ready to be at the center of everyone's attention. I suggest you take the time and build your style and have your style develop as your career develops. If you choose this method at the point you get to the head of the pack, your style will be ready, come what may.

STANDING OUT!

It will surprise you how many people put a great deal of effort into fitting in and feel standing out is the last thing they want to do. Some people would prefer not to be in the spotlight, nor do they want to feel forced to be the center of attention. Fact is, you cannot be successful without spending time in the spotlight. There are those who feel being put in a crowd keeps them safe and seek to blend in so it can possibly secure their place. These individuals think if they function without doing any more or less than those around them, this ensures their position within an organization. Fitting in is the strategy of many people in the workforce today, I have seen it with my own eyes and I must say if you plan on maintaining a position at a company for a long period of time, that go-along-to-get-along strategy just may work for you. But, if you plan to aim for the top, then standing out cannot be avoided, nor should it.

I read a book a gentleman wrote about fitting in at the workplace. He wrote this book for all those people who felt like they were outsiders while at work. So I researched this topic and through my research found many people struggle with fitting in at the workplace. As I encourage you to stand out, I understand this concept will be challenged by fear and the concerns many people have about fitting in. So I feel it's only fair to provide the pros and cons of being in the spotlight. No one said being successful was going to be easy or simple. There is a reason for the saying "it's lonely at the top". Let's be clear if you going to go through the intricate task of developing a style to complement your skills in order to position yourself for success. You will surely need to prepare yourself to stand alone, it is counter-intuitive to position yourself for success but be afraid to stand alone when necessary. I should be clear that I am not trying to encourage anyone to be a misfit, nor am I suggesting that you should not maintain a cohesive relationship with your colleagues and coworkers in the workplace. I strongly recommend being a team player and seek always to be celebrated as someone who can be counted upon.

What I am clearly defining is that you must use your skills and style to rise above mediocrity and stand in a class by yourself. When you find yourself in a class of your own, you will be celebrated by those who benefit the most from your good work, in other words, your boss, your clients, your customers, family, friends, loved ones, etc. But, you may be detested by those who benefit the least from your outstanding nature, to be exact, coworkers, colleagues, nemeses, competitors, phony friends, and ex-lovers. The popular term for this is called "the haters". So as you build your style to be something that is celebrated, you must also build your character to withstand the good, the bad and the ugly that come with the nature of standing alone among many.

APPEARANCE OF STYLE

"Life loves to be taken by the lapel and told, 'I'm with you kid. Let's go."
- Maya Angelou

"No matter what business you are in, you want to stand out and display the many aspects that make you exceptional."

GET THE WINNING EDGE!

Exactly what does your image say about who you are? In this fast-paced, technologically advanced society we live in, it may appear on the surface that your image should take a back seat to your knowledge. But truth be told, your image needs to be on a par with the knowledge you possess.

We live in a very competitive world where everyone is looking for an edge, a world where competition is often at the very heart of most business environments. Your image can be the distinct mechanism that will give you the edge you need to succeed; your image is the key component that will help you separate yourself from those who do and those who do it well. I can recall all the compliments and praise I received from colleagues and acquaintances who often commented on my appearance. They seem to be inspired and excited by my presentation and the manner in which I conducted myself. Now who wouldn't want to be inspired and feel embraced even before you start to get down to business? This is certainly the effect having the right appearance can have within any environment.

No matter what business you are in, you want to stand out and display the many aspects that make you exceptional. In a suit and tie environment, you can jazz up your standard blue and gray outfit by accessorizing with cufflinks, exceptional ties, unique socks, and braces for those who appreciate a classic look. You will be surprised how a little can go a long way. It is all about the details, paying attention to them will get you noticed faster than having on a new suit.

CAPTURE YOUR STYLE DNA!

Before you can start your journey on transforming your image from ordinary to extraordinary, you must create your own personal style. You must delve deep into your subconscious where you can create your style DNA. What is a style DNA, you might ask? Your style DNA is a process in which you do some soul searching; you will need to identify effectively your comfort levels, where you know exactly what you are comfortable wearing and what style represents you best. If you are dressed well, but feel uncomfortable, then you are doing something very wrong. Because the lack of comfort will show through your image and negatively influence your confidence. Once your confidence is shaken, it will become obvious to others around you that, although you are dressed well, you're not comfortable. And at that point your image is in jeopardy of being a negative as oppose to a positive one.

This reminds me of a time when I took notice of a gentlemen who was dressed very well. When someone is well put-together, I do not hesitate to compliment him or her. After some time had passed, I noticed the well-dressed gentlemen walking in the distance and the one thing that stood out the most--it even trumped his well-tailored suit was the obvious fact that his feet were hurting. He kept trying to adjust his feet in his shoes, but seemed to find no comfort. This is a clear example of why comfort is the highest priority when it comes to dressing well. In my observation, it was clear he was not comfortable, and no matter how well put-together this gentleman was, he could not disguise his extreme discomfort, which ultimately affected his ability to wear his clothing with confidence. We all know how it feels to have aching toes in uncomfortable shoes one time or another; this is not a good feeling, or a pretty sight in his case. On that day, his shoes got the best of him. It all comes down to how well your clothes fit you and how your clothes feel on you. Your clothes should always feel good on you and be worn with ease. Your garments ultimately should make you feel relaxed and complement your comfort level, which will certainly enhance your confidence level. It all should flow hand-in- hand, while one should never part from the other. Comfort is the foundation to any wardrobe. The best way to ensure comfort is to have your clothes tailored. I know the first thought most have when they hear someone say tailor, they immediately think of a boutique on Park or Madison Avenue with a gentleman who has a tape measure in one hand and straight pins in the other. This is partially true, but you can just take you garments to your local cleaners; they should have someone who can make alterations and adjustments to your garments just as well. At the end of the day, all that really matters is that your clothing fits you appropriately and you are comfortable wearing them. If I haven't stressed it enough, you do not want to sacrifice comfort for anything because you will not be able to wear your clothes effortlessly, which should be your ultimate goal.

It is important that you always dress the part; your appearance should complement your style and what you do for a living. The best way to instill confidence in others about who you are and what you do is by exceeding expectation in whatever it is you do. The same applies to your appearance; a pleasant surprise wins every time. I have a theory I call being on **All Fours,** you must **look the part**, **walk the part**, **talk the part** and ultimately **be the part**. If you effectively apply my theory of being on **All Fours,** then you will utilize your image to help inspire confidence in others and you will see how it can be a powerful tool.

Look Your Best!

Don't be like most and take looking your best for granted, because it is a key component to being your best. The bottom-line is this: your image is what people see first, so this is the primary impression that we utilize when first meeting someone. I had the opportunity to speak with a veteran recruiter with over a decade of staffing experience, De'Angelo James, who provided a deeper insight into how your image can impact your first impression.

Q: You have interviewed hundreds of people over the last ten years in your profession. Can you tell me just how important is the presentation of a potential candidate when being considered for a job opportunity?

A: It's highly important, because your first impression is everything. The first second that candidate walks through my door without intentionally thinking about it, I am scanning them from head to toe, and that is when they have an opportunity to first impress me without even saying a word yet. Understand that it is very rare to come across people on an interview these days that stands out from the norm clothing-wise, so when I get a candidate who does, it makes a difference

Q: What are the things that stand out and make a very good impression on you when first meeting potential hires?

A: First, are they dressed appropriately for the interview? This lets me know right from the start do they have a sense of awareness of the accepted dress code. You may not believe this, but I have interviewed people with master's degree or beyond who have come to an interview with jeans and loafers. Second, how well do they wear their clothing? I always notice a nice flashy tie, shoes, shirt socks, etc. when I first meet a person. I am sure others in my profession would agree that these are icebreakers that get us to warm up to the person who is being interviewed, and all employers appreciate a well put together candidate. It gives us a feeling of confidence and puts me in a position to compliment that person if done correctly and starts the interview on a good note. Although I don't always compliment a candidate on his attire, I always notice the effort, and that is more important than anything else.

Q: How does this affect your decision to hire the person?

A: Well I can't say that this is the deal closer, but I can say that a well-dressed candidate is easier to remember when determining my final decision after a month of interviews with several candidates. I have made notes in the past about something I like appearance-wise about a candidate that has kept him at the front of the list, assuming the interview went well also. I would leave off saying that whatever you can do to stand out within corporate acceptance would only add to your advantage in the end.

RELAX YOURSELF, NOT YOUR STYLE!

Let's make no bones about it: in this world we live in, you can call it many things, superficial or materialistic. But the reality is this--how you look and how you present yourself play a major role in others' perception of you, it is crucial to how people will receive you. The added benefit is the influence the right image can command. I can recall during my financial consultant days, as I traveled from one client to the next, working on various projects. The effect I had on any given environment became obvious; I had the ability to enhance and have a positive influence by being consistent with my image and the professionalism my presence promoted. In a short time, I noticed other individuals began to up their dress game. If this is an aspect of your life that you have control over, then obviously it is in your best interest to put your best foot forward. Don't you think?

Don't kid yourself. In an era I like to call the Post-Silicon Valley Khaki, when it comes to dressing for success, well, people have been rather lax. It is called the Post-Silicon Valley Khaki era because it is drawn from the 90's dress-down business environment, which was at first instituted by technology companies in Silicon Valley, the technology Mecca. This dressing down, which initially seemed like a good idea, burst into the new millennium and spread like wildfire, infecting other industries. It went to the point where the infected industries ranged from the financial businesses to the legal field. These fields, traditionally known to adhere to the strictest dress policies, were now adopting a more relaxed dress code. I knew there would be a problem when I saw financial companies adopting these same dress-down policies and establishing dress-down business weeks for their satellite offices.

Now there have always been industries where a relaxed work environment was commonplace; particularly the entertainment industry has always been a very liberal self-expressive industry, just as the advertising business has always cultivated a creative "easy does it" atmosphere. But when the technology industry became dominant in the 90's, the dress to impress ideology of days gone by went out the window. At that point, khakis and polo's became the workplace uniform in a wide range of fields. This relaxed trend, although popular, did not go without its share of criticism and adverse effect on business. Some studies have shown that there were many drawbacks from having a too relaxed work environment, such as employees having a more careless approach and attitude toward their work. These studies have shown an erosion of professionalism, which could be attributable to these relaxed work environments.

If you search the world, you will find that there is a universal dress standard. Whether you are in Europe, Asia, Africa or the Americas, you will see that in most business settings people adhere to the International Standard Business Attire. This is informal business attire. Keep in mind that it is called informal because international formal is deemed black tie affair formal, so technically a business suit and tie is called informal business attire. But it is better known as western business attire. There are a slew of other terms like business-casual or smart-casual, where you wear your suit but leave your tie at home. At the end of the day, a suit and tie still remain the standard acceptable business attire and this has not fundamentally changed, regardless of trends that seem to dominate certain regions of the world.

GUIDELINES OF STYLE
"What a fine man. Hath your tailor made you!"
- Philip Massinger

"The old adage "clothes don't make the man" is a true statement. The fact is, it takes a man of style to bring his clothes to life."

STYLE IS NEVER OUT OF STYLE!

When I started out my career on Wall Street, the power suit was all the rage; it was the blue pinstripe suit with a bold tie, which was a look everyone was trying to achieve, and the must-have accessory was a pair of braces (suspenders). Everyone had his own interpretation of how braces should be worn; some did the solid colors to offset the power tie, while others chose to find unique designs. Trafalgar makes the most outstanding designs, but there are other brands, so you need to explore and be on a quest for the best. The contrast between the ties and braces can be an awesome combination if you explore the many options and do not put too much thought into it. The main rule of thumb is the color family should always be the same; you can also add your pocket square to that combination. Although the style of wearing braces is a thing of the past by way of the 80's power look era, you should keep in mind that classic style is never out of style, so you can always include braces in your wardrobe every once in a while.

A sport jacket is this most versatile garment a man can have in his wardrobe, because it can just about be worn with anything as long as it is worn correctly. Right off the bat, you should know by now that the jacket must be tailored; it should fit well and be comfortable. Whether a solid color or patterned like hound's-tooth or check, it should be in a color that is wearable with the full range of your versatile wardrobe. In warmer weather you will have the opportunity to explore colors that should only be worn in the spring and summer, lighter shades and lighter weight fabrics. The all-time summer favorite has to be linen, and for the vacationing and leisure voyages a seersucker suit is an excellent choice, if you have the confidence to match the boldness and suppleness of this outfit. A sport jacket is sometimes referred to as a blazer, which is technically incorrect; the real distinction is that a blazer is a blue jacket, which is sometimes adorned with brass buttons. There is an interesting history to the blazer, and as you become a style connoisseur you should research the history of how various pieces of garments came about.

ONLY A STYLISH MAN CAN BREATHE LIFE INTO HIS CLOTHES.

The old adage "clothes don't make the man" is a true statement. The fact is, it takes a man of style to bring his clothes to life. Simply put, anyone, if he can afford it, could buy an expensive piece of clothing, but it is only the man with a personal sense of style who can animate his wardrobe. So for the person with a true sense of style, the man makes his clothes come alive and stand in a class of its own.

When it comes to cologne, chemistry plays a major part in how a fragrance smells on an individual. Two individuals can spray on the same cologne, but each would smell different. The same applies for wearing quality garments. The same exact suit will look different on the different individuals because the fit will not be the same. This is why tailoring is absolutely a must for most of the garments you will purchase off the rack. You would want the fit to compliment you in every way. It really does not matter what your size or shape is, the only thing that truly matters is that your clothes fit suitably. This means no slouching pants or pant legs dragging to the ground, no sport jacket sleeves down to the knuckles, which are all unacceptable. A tailor will fix these size and fit issues for a nominal fee and the result will be priceless. Finding a tailor is like finding the right barber: once you locate the one who can cut your hair without you saying a word, he will stay with you for a lifetime.

A GOOD TAILOR IS HARD TO FIND!

When choosing a tailor there is one thing you need to know: does he/she pay attention to details? There's nothing worse than having one pant leg hemmed slightly higher than the other, or one arm a little shorter. These are small imperfections that will bother you every single time you put on the article of clothing. A tailor who pays attention to every detail would never make this sort of blunder and would precisely measure you to ensure that the fit truly fits. The possibilities are endless when it comes to the use of a fine tailor. You can have him adjust any new garment you purchase, but you can also have him alter an old piece of clothing that you no longer wear due to weight fluctuation or a height adjustment. A good example would be having an old shirt adjusted that you no longer wear. In the mid 90's, a loose fitted shirt was the cut of the day; every designer was cutting shirts large for a loose fit. Whereas now, fitted shirts, with a European flair, is the cut of the day. Try having a tailor taper the side of an old shirt for a more fitted look. This will give new life to something old and save you some doe to boot.

I hope these tips are helpful and allow you to discover how being stylish, if done correctly, should not cost you a fortune, but certainly can make you look like you are worth a fortune.

SIDE-STEP OF STYLE
"The journey of a thousand miles begins with one step."
- Lao Tzu

"Creating your own personal style will have an enormous impact on your entire life."

IT ALL STARTS WITH BEING A GENTLEMAN FIRST.

Having a story to tell about your great finds makes the entire style experience enjoyable and rewarding. Too often in today's fast-paced environment, people don't take time or opportunity to have conversations, nor do we exchange pleasantries as we travel our journeys each day. Some people can be well dressed and appealing based on their outward appearance, but at the same time gives off an unapproachable aura.

People no longer engage in offering up a compliment or just a goodwill gesture toward their fellow man. We all need to embrace the practice of extending a compliment, especially when warranted, which should definitely enhance our quality of life.

You must be prepared to receive compliments from people who will be drawn to you when they encounter your unique sense of style. It would truly be ironic to be dressed well with a clearly defined sense of personal style, but do not want anyone to notice you or engage in a conversation with you. I hope that defining your personal style will include enhancing your personality as well as your interpersonal abilities, because ultimately all these factors will go hand and hand.

RE-ENGINEER YOURSELF!

Creating your own personal style will have an enormous impact on your entire life. It will attract liked-minded individuals with similar style consciousness and it will influence people to treat you in a particular manner. It can have a tremendous effect on the way you conduct your life as well. In essence, it will become your lifestyle, and this is truly an important factor, because that is exactly the effect you should be looking for.

You want your style to be comfortable and you want to wear your clothing with ease; you shouldn't feel like you are dressed up, nor should you feel like you need a special occasion to look presentable. When your style becomes a part of your lifestyle, than you will know what to wear and when to wear it at all times. Keep in mind, a large part of wearing clothing well and cementing your personal style is having the confidence to pull it off.

CONTEMPORARY FLAIR & CLASSIC STYLE!

One of the most important style principles you should adapt is the appreciation for a classic style, which, by the way, will never go out of style, especially if you merge contemporary flair with the traditionally classic pieces of clothing.

A pocket-handkerchief or a pair braces, even a hat, can add a classic look to your contemporary style. Bear in mind that the fusion of modern and classic panache will allow you to add new styles to your pre-existing wardrobe, which is the main purpose of creating your own style.

Also, it will allow adaptability to keep your look fresh and clean. You can always add a double-button, long collar shirt to your classic windowpane or pinstripe suit. It is highly recommended that you exercise often and stay fit for health reasons; additionally, being fit will afford you the opportunity wear your clothes well.

Many shirt manufacturers are making fitted shirts that are more streamlined than the traditional full cut shirts and the look is very clean. These enhancements will certainly accentuate your pre-existing style. Being healthy never hurt, either.

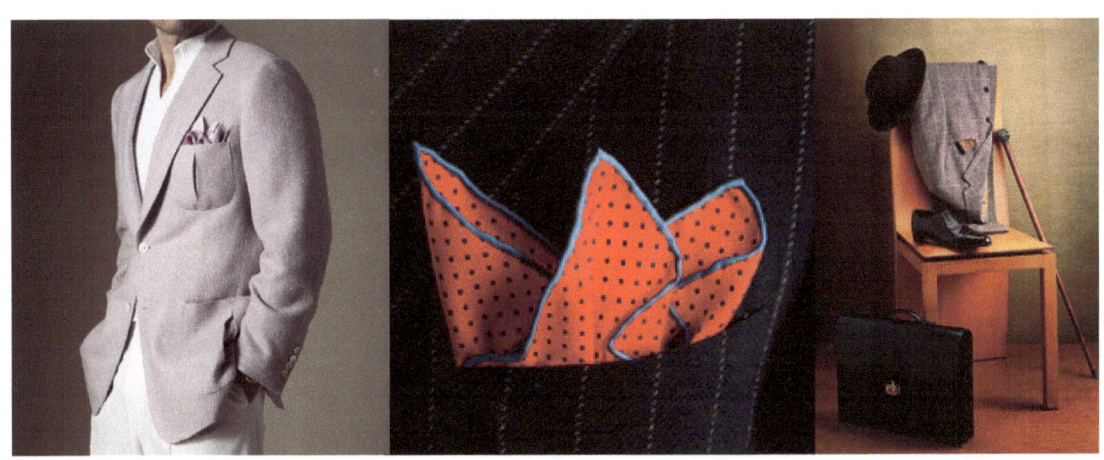

Don't Be Afraid to Show Your True Colors!

Acknowledgements

This book was a long time coming. I would say that it was a labor of love, but in reality it was a call to duty to share the information I've acquired over the years. I was encouraged to write this book and when I finally wrapped my head around the idea of putting my knowledge on paper in the form of a book, I must admit the task wasn't simple and the journey wasn't easy. So I must acknowledge all the individuals who have been instrumental in helping me through the journey in order for you to be reading these very words in this book.

I would be remiss if I didn't start with the very foundation of my existence, my heart, my soul, my joy: Demetria & Dmitri. My life is complete, and that is because of my family.

There is a void in my heart and that void is my son Malique. Although I did not have him with me during the writing of this book, he is with me in my heart at all times.

I'm going to keep it short as I thank my mother for her love and support because if I wrote about all that my mother have done for me, it would be a book unto itself. I will say with the strength of God on her side and the compassion of Jesus, she has loved and guided me throughout my life. All that you see and all that I am is the result of my mother's love, guidance, and time she invested in me. Thank you, Mom!

There is a person that is in a category of his own: my business partner, my friend, my brother, and the person who ignited the spark that fueled the fire by which this book was cast. De'Angelo James, you have supported me in many endeavor far beyond most, with the understanding and patience of a saint. You believed and supported me through thick & thin. For those reasons I want to thank you, Sir.

Being the youngest of five boys without any sisters had a tremendous impact on my outlook in life and shaped the very person I am. My four older brothers have affected me in that I can see a little of each one of them in me. John, Alaric, Terrell and Brian: Thank you for always letting me be the little brother that I am.

Aunt Julia, you have always been a loving supporter from near and from afar. Your friendship and sisterhood with Mom have continuously been present throughout my life. I want you to know that I thank you and love you.

To all of my extended family members: I hope this book will serve as a symbol of encouragement, which clearly becomes self evident that anything is possible if you are willing to do the impossible. I extend my love to you all.

There are so many other individuals who have been very supportive who are outside my immediate circle of family and close friends. It is too numerous to name everyone, but I cannot overlook the support of Anita Shari Peterson, Steve Krampf, Marcus Knight, Jennifer Hubbard, Shaunice Hawkins, and tremendous support as well as encouragement from Ms. Terrie M. Williams. Each of you provided a source of support and inspiration. Thank you.

I must acknowledge Kenneth Salikof for providing his editing expertise and for having the patience and understanding necessary to work with a novice author. Thank you, sir.

When I think about how I would like this book to affect the world, I can't help but think of my apprentice Dorian Sermon. This would be the best example of a young man who has all the potential to do great things, and armed with the right tools and information there is no stopping you and all the millions of young adults like you. Remember the plan: do what you got to do in order to do what you want to do.

I have a motto that I live by; it's my take-one-day-at-a-time exercise. I encourage everyone to try it. I breathe, I smile, and I live.

index

A
A Pair of Shoes 1887, 23
Accessories, 8, 42, 46, 47
Appearance, 10, 72, 76, 77, 80, 81, 88, 90, 92, 94, 95, 103, 105, 106, 114

B
Baggy Jeans, 67
Blazer, 67, 69, 89, 109
Brown Shoes, 30, 67
Business Suit, 73, 97, 107
Belt, 8, 19, 33, 37, 46, 51, 95
Business, 7, 9, 24, 27, 28, 58, 73, 74, 75, 76, 88, 91, 92, 97, 99, 103, 107
Braces, 15, 25, 36, 37, 103, 109, 115

C
C.S. Lewis, 65
Casual Trousers, 73
Coats, 12
Collared dress shirt, 73
Comfortable, 7, 8, 16, 33, 37, 66, 68, 83, 89, 95, 105, 109, 114
Confident, 8
Contemporary Flair, 115
Cool, 8, 68, 69
Cufflinks, 8, 12, 34, 35, 47, 91, 103
Complimentary, 9
Colors, 16, 18, 26, 28, 33, 35, 36, 61, 83, 95, 96, 99, 109, 116
Cuts, 16
Collars, 18
Classic Style, 25, 49, 109, 115
Craftsmanship, 27
Casual, 9, 21, 28, 34, 60, 65, 66, 67, 69, 73, 75, 76, 88, 95, 96, 97, 99, 107

D
Dressing Well, 7, 76, 77, 91, 105
Designers, 11, 12
Dressing Appropriately, 9, 25
Dress Down, 107
Designs, 21, 28, 35, 36, 37, 59, 61, 95, 109
Dress Code, 73, 75, 89, 106, 107

Department Store, 12, 26
Dress shoes, 57

E
Egyptian Cotton, 18
European Cut, 27, 111

F
Fitted Shirt, 61
Fashion, 6, 10, 11, 12, 14, 15, 16, 24, 43
Fashionable, 12, 43
Fabric, 18, 33, 47, 52, 94, 95, 96, 109
Footwear, 24, 26, 28, 68

G
GQ Magazine, 11
Gentlemen, 26, 94, 105
Garments, 6, 7, 16, 50, 74, 105, 109, 110

H
Hat collection, 8, 40, 42, 43, 44, 68, 69
Hand-Made, 6, 10, 12, 17, 19, 21, 26, 27, 28, 34, 35, 53, 72, 75, 88, 95, 105, 114, 115
Handsome, 27, 28
Hosiery, 34, 35, 36, 50

I
Introduction, 5, 6
If not, why?, 83
If so, why? 83

J
Jeans, 28, 67, 68, 69, 76, 89, 94, 96, 106

M
Miles Davis, 64
Men's Boutique, 12, 24, 26, 53
Measurement, 27
Manufacturer, 27, 28, 115
Maintenance, 7, 28

O

Oversized, 67. 69
Oversized T-Shirt, 67
Occasion, 6, 9, 28, 40, 43, 60, 73, 74, 75, 84, 89, 91, 92, 114
Opportunities, 8, 90

P

Philip Massinger, 108
Pocket Handkerchief, 12, 30, 35
Personal Stylist, 7
Professional Attire, 9
Power Suit, 15, 109
Power Tie, 15, 109
Power Lunch, 15
Paisley, 21
Powerful Presentation, 28
Personal Style, 6, 8, 22, 33, 35, 46, 84, 105, 112, 114
Polo Shirt, 95, 96, 97
Psychology, 78, 80, 84

R

Ralph Waldo Emerson, 17
Rule 007, 73
Re-Engineer Yourself, 114

S

Shirts, 7, 12, 14, 18, 19, 21, 52, 99, 111, 115
Shoes, 7, 8, 9, 12, 18, 21, 22, 24, 26, 27, 28, 33, 46, 48, 50, 51, 67, 68, 73, 86, 88, 91, 95, 105, 106
Slim Cut, 61
Socks, 8, 11, 32, 33, 50, 53, 103, 106
Specialty Shop, 12
Sport coat, 46, 66, 73
Style DNA, 66, 82, 83, 89, 105
Suits, 7, 9, 10, 12, 15, 19, 30, 43, 60, 66, 97
Sweaters, 12
Stylish, 10, 12, 22, 24, 26, 28, 37, 43, 52, 61, 64, 68, 72, 73, 76, 110, 111
Self-Expression, 10
Sport Jacket, 18, 97, 109, 110
Slacks, 18, 28, 36, 37, 89, 95, 96, 99
Steam Press, 19
Sartorial, 21
Style-Trademark, 22
Super 120's, 21, 26
Style Connoisseur, 46, 109
Successful, 7, 82, 90, 92, 99, 101

T

The Anatomy of my Style, 10, 16
Texture, 28, 33, 95, 96
Tailor, 26, 31, 36, 37, 47, 105, 108, 109, 110, 111
Timepiece, 8, 56, 58, 60, 62
Technology, 36, 107
Ties, 8, 9, 12, 14, 15, 16, 21, 54, 66, 68, 74, 76, 77, 90, 94, 96, 103, 109, 111, 114
Trousers, 12, 36, 37, 50, 73
Tuxedo, 73

U

Universal Dress Code, 73, 75

V

Vincent van Gogh, 23

W

Wardrobe, 6, 7, 8, 9, 11, 14, 15, 19, 21, 22, 24, 26, 28, 33, 36, 37, 42, 43, 50, 66, 74, 76, 88, 92, 94, 96, 97, 105, 109, 110, 115
Wall Street, 15, 36, 38, 60, 109
Well-dressed, 10, 11, 77, 91, 105, 114
Workmanship, 27, 28
Well-made, 42, 68

Resource guide

Andrew's Ties USA
400 Madison Ave.
New York, NY 10017
212-750-5221
andrewstieusa.com

B. Oyama.NY
2330 7th Avenue
New York, NY 10030
212-234-5128
boyamany.com

Beau Brummel
347 West Broadway
New York, NY 10013
212-219-2666

Botticelli
522 5th Avenue
New York, NY 10036
212-768-1430
botticellishoes.com

Berluti Shoes
31 Rue Marbeuf
75008 Paris France
+33 01 53 53 1100
berluti.com

Cesare Attolini
Via Visconti di Modrone
19 Milano 20121
+39 02 763 16 757
cesareattolini.com

Charles Tyrwhitt
98-100 Jermyn Street
London, SW1Y 6EE
+44 0 20 7839 6060
ctshirts.com

Corneliani S.p.A.
Via Panizza, 5
46100 Mantova
+39 03 763 04 429
corneliani.com

Domenico Vacca
781 5th Avenue
New York, NY 10022
212-759-6333
Domenicovacca.com

Hackett London
87 Jermyn Street
London, SW1Y 6JD
+44 0 20 7930 1300
hackett.com

Isaia
Via Tortona, 35
20144 Milano
+39 02 773 31 502
isaia.it

Oxxford Clothes
717 5th Avenue
New York, NY 10022
212-593-0911
oxxfordclothes.com

Pal Zileri
Via Fabio Filzi, 34
36050 Quinto Vicentino
+39 04 443 56 096
palzileri.it

Paul Stuart
Madison Ave. at 45th St.
New York, NY 10017
212-682-0320
paulstuart.com

Ralph Lauren
867 Madison Avenue
New York, NY 10021
22-606-2100
ralphlauren.com

Salvatore Ferragamo
655 5th Avenue
New York, NY 10022
212-759-3822
ferragamo.com

Thomas Pink Shirts
1 Palmerston Court
London, SW8 4Aj
+44 020 7498 3882
thomaspink.com

Tom Ford
845 Madison Avenue
New York, NY 10021
212-359-0300
tomford.com